PENGUIN BOOKS

YOU ARE NOT A ROCK

Mark Freeman is a mental health coach and human-centered design workshop facilitator based in Toronto. He has taught Shakespeare's plays in Korea, tended gardens in Spain, filmed an Arabic-language documentary on youth employment in Cairo, and facilitated strategy workshops for executives at multiple Fortune 500 companies. After recovering from several mental illness diagnoses, he now focuses on leveraging technology and design to help people around the world navigate the complex changes necessary to improve and maintain great mental health and fitness. He is the cofounder of the online mental health community Everybody Has a Brain, and he is a Stanford Medicine X ePatient Scholar. His favorite pastimes include sitting and breathing.

Thank you to everybody who's tolerated my stumbling around on this journey. Thank you for offering shelter, feeding me cookies, and sharing your knowledge about how to cross the rivers ahead.

CONTENTS

Part Two: The Transformation   *151*

YOU ARE
NOT A ROCK

INTRODUCTION

I HAVE A BRAIN

Ten years ago, if you'd told me I'd be writing a book about overcoming mental illness and building better mental health, I would have said you were crazy. I didn't know anything about mental health, and I certainly didn't have a mental illness. But I was very wrong.

By the time I was in my late twenties, reality was increasingly something with which I struggled. Whenever I left my apartment, I'd go through a series of rituals to check the stove, stand in front of it, check that appliances were off, that they didn't feel hot, unplug anything I could unplug, check that the windows were locked, and then, finally, leave the apartment. Then I'd lock the front door, check that the front door was locked, and debate with myself about whether my memory of checking the stove moments earlier actually came from a few moments ago or the day before. I'd leave, then come back to check that my laptop was hidden under my bed so thieves wouldn't find it, and then, realizing that the curtains were open, I'd close them because the thieves might have seen where I hid my laptop. Then I'd take it from under my bed and put it in my closet under some clothes before leaving the building by a different door from the one I came in by (to trick the thieves who were watching me). But then I'd go back to check the lock again because I was so focused on my escape route, I couldn't remember if I'd locked the front door, and as I was already back at the

1

apartment, why not check the stove again, the back door, maybe the toaster, check if there was anything near any of the plugs that could catch fire, and then jiggle the door again on the way out, then once more because the first time might have unlocked it. I'd finally peel myself away, preoccupied with imaginary conversations in my head between me and people I was upset with at school because of something that had almost happened the day before.

When I walked upstairs, I would see myself falling and splitting my jaw apart on the steps, teeth scattering everywhere. The bones in my face would ache like it had actually happened.

When I was standing at an intersection, I would see cars run right over the pedestrians in the crosswalk, splashing guts and bones across the road in front of me. I would feel like I was going to vomit.

I saw violent things happen to other people or me all of the time, and the violence was often my fault. I was afraid to carry knives in the kitchen if anybody else was around because I would see myself stabbing them. I couldn't carry a knife in the kitchen if my roommate's cat, Glick, was there because I'd see the knife go right through Glick's head. If I was cutting vegetables, I'd feel my fingers getting sliced off.

Reality was a subjective, viscerally painful experience. I developed stereotypical symptoms of obsessive compulsive disorder (OCD), like repeatedly washing my hands under scalding hot water, along with lesser-known symptoms, like checking my ID repeatedly and wondering if the person pictured on it was actually me. I was convinced I would someday hand it to a police officer and get thrown in jail because I was impersonating somebody. And these are only a tiny selection of the extreme end of the symptoms with which I struggled. Most of the time, I was just drowning in anxiety for no particular reason.

But I didn't even think any of that was strange. When I first went to see a counselor, all I told her was that I was having some depression and sex issues. I had no idea why. In any situation, my brain would immediately jump to the worst, most violently gruesome outcomes imaginable. I spent all of my time and energy either ruminating or trying to find somebody to hook up with (but then not actually meeting them because of my insecurities and health anxieties). Those were the only problems in my life. I was very smart. I was not crazy.

I got a bunch of mental illness labels stuck on me as I stumbled through the system: OCD, generalized anxiety disorder (GAD), depression, and addiction. Those labels were as much about each therapist's areas of expertise as they were about what I was aware of or willing to share.

The specific symptoms I struggled with might make for great suffertainment or illness porn—everybody loves to gawk at a good car crash as they creep by on the freeway of life—but I swear that the far more interesting journey is the journey of being healthy. I no longer struggle with any of those diagnoses. This is not a book about my past. This is not a book about *having* mental illness. We'll get into some more of the symptoms I dealt with, but if you're looking for a confessional memoir about a lifetime spent managing and suffering from mental illness, this is not the book for you.

WHOM IS THIS BOOK FOR?

I've had to take a relatively extreme journey from being very sick to being very healthy, like the mental health equivalent of somebody who goes from being dangerously out of shape to running marathons. What I've learned on that journey can help anybody who's interested in taking care of her mental health and preventing a journey like the one I had to take.

We won't explore instant, mystical secrets to overcoming mental health challenges. Mental health and fitness are hard work, just like physical health and fitness. Changing your brain takes time and effort, like changing any other part of your body. I am not going to share with you any magical supplements or special mantras. I'm not going to tell you to burn all of your possessions and trek into the rain forest in a loincloth to chew some roots while you rub an iguana on your forehead. I've never taken any medication for my mental health, so I don't have a perfect chemical to share or a gene for you to blame for your problems. This is simply a book about actions. If you're ready to develop practices in your life that will help you handle difficult experiences as you take action to do things you care about, then this book is for you.

HOW THIS BOOK WORKS

This book is divided into two sections. The first section is all about learning basic mental health skills and unlearning the ways of thinking and behaving that cause mental health challenges in our lives. The second section is all about making the switch from a fear-fueled, anxiety-driven life to one that's based on your values, that's about creating and building what you want to see in the world instead of trying to avoid and control what you don't want to see.

At the end of all of the chapters except for the last one, you'll find an exercise. **Do the exercises.** When you do the exercises in this book, not only will they become more useful to you but you'll be able to engage more with the content of the book because we'll have shared experiences of tackling challenges together.

Some of the exercises we'll cover are there to help you support changes in your life. They're human-centered design and change management exercises adapted from the business world. Improving and maintaining great mental health and fitness is a big, complex innovation in your life. It's similar to complex changes companies are making all of the time to successfully innovate. We can apply the same tools to innovate in our own lives.

FAIL

As with physical fitness, failing is part of improving your emotional fitness. If you find the exercises in this book difficult, that's awesome! If you fail at them, great! Keep going.

With any of the concepts or exercises we cover, test them out, play around with them, get them to work in your life. Focus on what works to help you with the challenges you're overcoming.

Those moments that feel impossible are actually when change happens. In a sense, taking on challenges is impossible with the brain or the body we have, but pushing through them in a healthy way changes us, and we develop the body and brain we *need* to make overcoming those challenges possible.

Have you ever done a burpee? It's a deceptively cute-sounding exercise. To do one, you drop your chest to the ground, push up into a plank, jump your feet forward to your hands, then jump up in the air, clap your hands over your head, drop back down into a plank, and bring your chest to the floor again. Repeat.

Developed in the 1930s by Royal Burpee as a fitness test, this simple exercise can quickly get exhausting. At the gym I attend, the workout of the day sometimes includes fifty burpees as a warm-up. There was a time when fifty burpees sounded like a complete workout to me, not a warm-up. If I had tried to do fifty burpees, I would have failed. I would've ended up with my head between my legs, gasping for breath and trying not to vomit. But now, because I've failed through many workouts with burpees, I can do them. All of the failures helped me get to a point where fifty burpees are a warm-up. This is as relevant to mental health and emotional fitness as it is to physical fitness. The capacity to do anything is on the other side of failure. Even with practicing skills like meditation or mindfulness, which we'll get to in the first half of the book, if you're new to them, expect to fail often at them. That's the only way they'll become useful supports in your life.

Those anxiety-ridden experiences of failure can become ways to measure progress, not by decreasing them, but by increasing them. Instead of letting anxieties and uncertainties fence off your life, they can become signposts showing you where to turn to do what actually matters to you.

If you avoid sweating, eventually everything makes you sweat. If you avoid anxiety, eventually everything makes you anxious.

SUPPORT YOUR EMOTIONAL FITNESS PRACTICE

I define emotional fitness as your capacity to experience emotions while continuing to make choices aligned with your values. It's analogous to cardiovascular fitness. It's an indicator of your ability to keep taking steps toward your goals in life while experiencing whatever emotions you're experiencing. It's not about avoiding feelings and controlling feelings. It's actually about feeling much more.

There are fundamentals to improving your physical fitness, regardless of the exercise. It's about finding that moment of discomfort, feeling it, believing it means you can't go further, knowing you need to stop, but then pushing through. Keep that in mind with emotional fitness.

When you embark on any process of complex change, like improving your physical or emotional fitness, it's important to gather supports in your life for that journey. Here are a few supports that can help you with implementing the changes we'll explore:

A recovery-focused therapist

It's so important for any therapist you work with to have a focus on recovery and helping you do the things you want to do in life. If you have a therapist who says you've got a chronic disease and all you can ever do is manage it, that's like asking a personal trainer to help you train for a marathon and him telling you it's not possible, you'll never be able to run a marathon, nobody does that, none of his clients has ever done that, he can't do that, so don't even try, the most you can hope to do is manage the symptoms of being out of shape, have you tried diet pills?

Personally, I wouldn't recommend working with that personal trainer. I wouldn't recommend working with a similar health-care practitioner. If you work with a professional on your fitness goals, whatever they may be, make sure that professional has a demonstrated track record of helping his patients to achieve the goals you're pursuing.

Peer support

Connect with people on similar journeys to your own. They might have done the journey at a different time, or taken a slightly different route, but they'll have insights into the challenges ahead of you and, most important, how to overcome them.

No matter how unique you may think your struggle is, many people have overcome the exact same issues, and many people are doing the work to overcome them right now, all around you. Connect with them.

Food

You run on energy. Whether you're a human, a robot, or a tomato plant, you need energy to do anything. If you're doing a strenuous activity, you need *more* energy. Making changes in your life is an incredibly strenuous activity. So fuel that practice. You can't have mental health without food.

It's important to note here that food can easily become wrapped up in the types of behaviors that make mental health worse. As we explore those behaviors throughout the book, consider how they apply to the way you eat. Watch out for trying to use food as a magic pill to solve mental health challenges. If you think you've discovered a too-good-to-be-true diet that promises to make anxiety and depression disappear, it's far more likely that all you've discovered is a potential eating disorder to slap on top of your existing issues.

Eat to fuel being yourself and doing what you love.

Exercise

Exercise is another support, similar to food, that you can do in a way that either benefits your mental health or makes it worse. Again, I want to emphasize that exercise is not a replacement for the changes that need to happen. You can be in amazing physical shape while also struggling with serious mental health challenges. When we start thinking we just need to exercise more and that's going to fix the problems in our life, we're slipping back into a trap of searching for a magic pill that will solve all of our problems.

Sleep

You have to sleep. Not only is it necessary for everyday functioning, but particularly when you're doing something like changing your brain—which is what we're going to be doing throughout this book—you need to sleep. Let your brain flush out all of the toxins that build up in there during the day. Let it take the time to build new connections. Let all of the things you're learning get settled in there. Sleep helps you handle your emotions better. You can be less reactive and less disturbed by things that normally might bother you. As we get into exercises to practice accepting feelings or thoughts that you might have avoided in the past, having enough sleep will help to make that a little bit easier.

Your breath

This is the most important support you'll need on this journey. Your breath is your unbreakable tether to the present. You'll often forget that it's there but you can always find it again, right where you left it. Come back to it when you encounter a challenge or when you meet something beautiful or when you take a step. If you notice you're floating off into the past or the future, follow your breath back to the path.

BE EMPOWERED

Take responsibility for making changes and empower yourself to make them. Recognizing that you can make changes to improve and maintain your mental health is not about blaming yourself for mental health challenges you're experiencing. It's about giving you back power that anxiety and fear have taken away. You can make changes that will help you be yourself and do the things you want to do in life.

I was very lucky when I finally found great therapists. One of the reasons I was so lucky is that they never suggested that I couldn't get over the challenges with which I was struggling. They expected recovery and they gave me the tools to recover.

When I hear people say that mental illness is chronic, it's as strange to me as if there were people standing outside of a gym shouting: "Exercise is a sham! You'll be out of shape forever! You'll only injure your knees! You're slow because you have a chemical imbalance! You don't have the genes for exercising so don't bother trying it!"

We know how to help people get into great physical shape. You can go to any gym and see people who have access to the skills and knowledge to do that. We're already at the same point with recovery from mental illness. People recover from OCD, they recover from schizophrenia, they recover from borderline personality disorder (BPD), they recover from eating disorders, they recover from depression, they recover from addiction. But, just like with physical fitness, it doesn't happen through magic. You have to work at it. However, not everybody succeeds at it. I'm sharing this book with you so that you will be more prepared to take on this challenge.

Feeling empowered to make a change can still seem like a daunting task. But one of the most beneficial lessons I learned on my own journey was that I could make changes everywhere, even with seemingly normal, everyday activities. With the first exercise we'll dive into you'll get to see how an activity you do many times daily (possibly more than a hundred times each day) can be an opportunity to make changes that support your mental health. This exercise is an excellent way to recognize how we practice patterns of behavior in our everyday lives, like reacting to uncertainties and urges in our heads, which can become problematic when those uncertainties are especially disturbing or those urges are pushing us to do things we want to stop. This exercise covers so many of the fundamentals that we'll build upon in the chapters ahead.

EXERCISE: Learn How to Catch an Urge

The most basic mental fitness skill is learning how to catch an urge, accept it, and then make a conscious, mindful decision about what you want to do. Everything we practice after this is simply an extension of accepting your internal experience and making a healthy decision. If you can master this skill, your productivity at work and school, your ability to pay attention to the people you care about, your ability to make decisions that support your romantic relationships, and your ability to use your free time in a way that makes you feel good about yourself can all improve. You'll be able to handle whatever pops into your head, keep your attention where you want to keep it, and make choices to build long-term health and happiness instead of reacting impulsively to short-term discomfort.

One of the simplest ways to practice this exercise is with your cell phone (but you can adapt it to anything you do automatically, like checking things on your computer, automatically turning on the TV when you get home, etc.). Here's how it works:

1. **Carry your phone with you at all times.** There's nothing wrong with having a phone on you. It's how you interact with it that causes problems.

2. **Experience the urge to check your phone.** Maybe you want to see if you received a text message you were waiting for, check for a response to an important e-mail, fill some time because you're bored, or flip through a dating app to find "the one." Whatever it is, don't try to get rid of the urge, but also DON'T CHECK YOUR PHONE! Feel the uncertainty. So much of improving your mental health is about learning to handle uncertainty and other feelings you don't like.

3. **Choose when you want to check your phone.** This is about putting you back in charge of how you spend your time and energy. Urges don't have to dictate your actions. You are not a dog. You do not have to chase every stick your brain throws at you. When you notice the urge to check, accept that urge—it's totally fine for it to be there— but pick the time and place when you'll check. And then follow through on that, whether or not you feel you need to when that time arrives.

4. **Practice.** Keep practicing until you no longer check your phone as a reaction to the urge to check. Use your phone only when you choose to use it. You may need to practice this exercise for a week or two before it begins to get normal. But go back to reacting to the urges your brain throws at

you only if compulsively reacting to urges is something at which you hope to become incredibly skilled.

If you don't feel you have a problem with checking your phone, or if it's not something that bothers you, that's great. This should be very easy for you then. But try this exercise before you decide it's not a struggle for you. If you can learn how to handle a simple uncertainty, like "Did I get an e-mail?" you'll be much more prepared to handle a big uncertainty, like "Should I end this relationship?" or "What if I'm about to die?" If you find that not checking your phone causes you noticeable discomfort or that you check it so automatically you don't even notice quickly enough to stop yourself, keep an open mind to the possibility that there are other behaviors in your life you're un-aware of that are contributing to poor mental health and fitness.

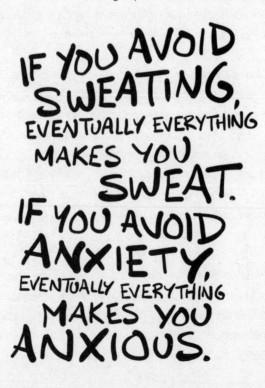

IF YOU AVOID SWEATING, EVENTUALLY EVERYTHING MAKES YOU SWEAT. IF YOU AVOID ANXIETY, EVENTUALLY EVERYTHING MAKES YOU ANXIOUS.

PART ONE

The Basics

Understand that you are not a rock

I want to share a true story with you. It's about some rocks. And it goes like this:

One day, early in the twenty-first century, up on a mountain in the Italian Alps, there were two very large rocks. They sat on the side of a mountain, overlooking a farm on the road between Ronchi and Cortaccia, Strada Provinciale 19 (in case you're planning a road trip).

On that particular day, there were external, contextual factors affecting the rocks, factors over which they had no control. Those contextual factors caused a landslide. And the rocks fell off the mountain.

They tumbled down the slope toward the farm. There was a single-lane country road at the bottom of the slope running alongside the farmhouse and the adjoining barn. One of the rocks landed on the road and stopped directly in front of the entrance to the farmhouse. It was a massive rock. It reached up to the roof of the farmhouse. With some extra momentum, it would have destroyed the house and everything (including everybody) inside.

The other, similarly enormous rock, however, didn't stop at the road. It rolled right across it, into the three-hundred-year-old barn on the other side. The force of the impact destroyed the barn, scattering wall planks and whole sections of the roof across the yard. The rock continued on down into the valley, getting an inefficient head start on the annual wine pressing, coming to rest beside an even larger rock that had fallen off the mountain many years before.

If rocks could feel, how do you think that rock would have felt after it did that? Embarrassed? Guilty? Desperate to blame the landslide? Angry at the other rock for not following through on their plan? Do you think that other rock was obsessing about the carnage it would have caused if it hadn't stopped?

How would you have felt if you were either of those rocks? Have you ever spent an hour thinking about what to write in a text message because you were afraid of saying the wrong thing and ruining a relationship? Have you reread and rewritten work e-mails over and over again, anxious about getting fired or seeming incompetent? Does responsibility make you anxious? Do you spend days obsessing about mistakes in your past? Do you wish you could get rid of those memories? Do you hear people in your head shouting at you for screwing up? Do you spend hours trying to rationalize why you're not to blame for things going wrong in your life?

So here's my point: Those are all very human experiences. Those rocks in that valley in Italy will never have any of those experiences. I said "*If* rocks could feel." They can't, they're rocks. You are not a rock. You feel things.

BE HUMAN

You probably approach physical fitness like a human. If you want to build strength, you lift heavy things that make you feel weak. If you want to increase endurance, you run until you're sweating and aching and ready to stop, and you keep running a little bit farther so that next time it won't be so difficult. If you want to be more flexible, you stretch into stiffness again and again until your flexibility increases. You try to go beyond last week's limits. You fail and fail and call it practice. You do squats and dead lifts until your legs are wobbly and so sore the next day that you can't sit down on the toilet, and you call that a good workout.

This paradoxical practice of doing the difficult thing so that the difficult thing isn't difficult is how humans change. This is a concept most people understand. If you told somebody that you plan to become stronger by avoiding strenuous exercise, even people who don't exercise would know that's ridiculous.

But there are probably many people around you who encourage you to approach mental health in the exact opposite way. They tell you not to do the difficult things. Avoid anxiety, feel less stress, don't think bad thoughts, watch out for triggers, get rid of uncertainty, man up, don't be so emotional, don't feel bad (everything will be okay). This is not how humans develop abilities to handle difficult challenges. Trying to avoid difficult things makes difficult things more difficult.

This is so important to understand as you get started on building better emotional fitness. You can develop your ability to handle emotions by feeling more, especially by feeling more of the feelings that challenge you. By lifting heavy emotions, lifting heavy emotions becomes easier. You can feel a greater range of emotions and you can feel them more deeply.

Poor mental health doesn't fall from the sky. Mental illness is like heart disease—you work your way up to it through a complex mix of environmental, genetic, and educational factors combined with each decision you make at home, at work, at school, and in relationships wherever you might be, every single minute of the day. Turning away from feelings, or trying to control them, cover them up, or chase after them, are the deep-fried pepperoni sticks, triple-decker cheeseburgers, and supersized routines of the mental health world. Sure, you might crave them, and they'll feel good, and you'll never be able to blame a specific junk food for giving you a heart attack, but when they become a regular part of your everyday life, the results are always nasty.

In the first two chapters, I'll cover two concepts that are fundamental to building better mental health and emotional fitness. It's important that we have a shared idea about what exercises for mental health look like and why we do them. So I'll repeat:

You are not a rock. You feel things.

I WANTED TO BE A ROCK

In the past, I constantly chose to do things inside my head and outside of it not to feel things. I didn't want to feel uncertain, or hated, or alone, or broke, or trapped, or ugly, or hurt, or unhappy, or guilty, or anxious. . . . There were so many feelings I didn't want to feel! I basically wanted to be a rock.

Rocks don't have varying levels of improvable mental health. Rocks don't imagine stabbing other rocks. Rocks don't get jealous or struggle with their sexuality or question the meaning of existence. Rocks don't convince themselves that other rocks are trying to poison them.

When we're trying not to feel things, we're trying to be rocks. So it's not surprising that we sink the moment we're thrown into uncertainty. Rocks sink.

Rocks will always feel less anxiety than you do. They will beat you every single time at feeling less guilt and regret. No rock will ever make as many mistakes as you will. No matter how much you practice meditation, you will always be more easily distracted and less focused than the most mediocre pebble in a muddy ditch. You will never worry as little as a rock worries. You will never be able to suppress your cravings as well as a rock does. No rock will ever relapse as many times as you do. No rock will ever fail as many times as you fail.

As you work through the exercises in this book and you live your life, remember that rock in that vineyard in Italy not thinking or feeling about the antique barn it obliterated. You are not like that rock. You cannot be like that rock. You can spend your entire life trying to be

like that rock but you'll only make yourself more miserable and you'll probably destroy much more than a barn.

You cannot build better mental health by trying to avoid being human. If you want to improve your mental health, it won't happen through wanting to avoid uncertainty, anxiety, and all of the other feelings you don't like. It'll happen by learning how to have those experiences. If you want to avoid human experiences, this is not the book for you. If you continue to pursue escape from those experiences, you will have only more of them, at ever-increasing levels of severity and complexity.

WHAT IS YOUR GOAL?

We often set goals for ourselves that might be better suited for rocks than for humans. We want to feel less anxiety, less guilt, less sadness; we want to obsess less, engage in compulsions less, be less lonely, less paranoid. . . . But we will never be able to do any of those things as well as rocks do. Have you ever seen a rock addicted to drugs or gambling? I haven't, either. Rocks are so disciplined!

Understanding that I am not a rock frames how I approach every mental health issue in my life. As a human, I can feel and think things I don't like. Translating this understanding into actions has been an incredible support for overcoming mental illness and continuing to improve my mental health. In particular, it shapes the goals I pursue. For you, with your mental health and even with this book, I strongly recommend that you **DON'T PURSUE GOALS THAT ROCKS CAN DO BETTER THAN YOU.**

Avoiding unhappiness is not the same as experiencing happiness. You can pour the rest of your life into trying not to be anxious and trying to prevent your worries from coming true, and all you'll have done is focused your energy on things that didn't even happen and you didn't even want to think about. Use this book to do things that rocks can't do better than you. And to help you with doing that, use the next exercise to set some creative human goals. These will be goals to keep in mind throughout the rest of the book and beyond. Each chapter ahead will help equip you with the knowledge and the skills to achieve these goals. But as you take steps toward your goals, always reflect on this question: Am I trying to do something that a rock can do better than me?

EXERCISE: Creative Human Goals

Rocks can do anything less than you can. But they can't do anything more than you can. So rather than setting goals around what you want to avoid, it helps to set goals around the things you'll build and create. Health is creative, not destructive. That doesn't mean we don't eliminate barriers like compulsive behaviors that get in the way of achieving our goals, but eliminating barriers isn't the end state. Unhealthy behaviors simply become things we don't do anymore because we're spending our time and energy on creating health and happiness and a life that's aligned with our values.

So grab something to write with and some paper and articulate creative human goals for yourself that rocks can't do better than you. Here are a couple of ideas to help you with this:

- If you had one overarching goal for your entire life, what would it be? If you looked at the different areas in your life, like health, relationships, work, education, etc., what would your goal be for each? What would your goal be for today? What's your goal for this moment right now? Take a look at the examples below comparing goals for rocks and goals for humans to see some possible directions for your goals:

GOALS FOR ROCKS	GOALS FOR HUMANS
I'll use this book to learn how to get rid of anxiety so I can finally start doing things I care about.	I'll use this book to learn how to handle more anxiety while I do things I care about.
Not be lonely anymore.	Attend at least one group social event every week.
I don't want people to judge me.	Be more accepting of others out on the street and online.
Stop feeling so much guilt and regret.	Learn how to practice feeling compassion toward myself and others.
Get rid of this uncertainty about whether my partner loves me.	Practice expressing myself honestly in a relationship even when I'm afraid of being hurt.

- In any situation it's possible to have a goal you're working toward, even if that goal is simply to breathe. The goals we carry into a situation shape our expectations. Whether our experience aligns with our expectations determines whether we laugh, shout, or cry. So what is your goal with this book? Did you pick up this book in the hope of getting rid of a feeling?

Because every rock is already much better than you when it comes to not experiencing that feeling. What's something that only you can do? What's something that you care about that you want to do more of in your life? How will you know if you've achieved that goal?

- Make sure your goals are visible. Put them where you'll see them. You might want to write them out on individual pieces of paper so you can put relevant goals where they're more likely to remind you to take action. If you have a goal to sleep more, maybe you need to stick that to your computer so you re-member to go to sleep earlier. Take your work goals with you to work. If you have a goal to improve your capacity to experience anxiety, where can you put that goal, physically or digitally, as a reminder to push into anxiety instead of avoiding it?

Recognize your problems

Most of my anxieties were linked with uncertainty and feeling uncomfortable. The amount of time and effort it took to avoid these feelings inevitably led to missing out on a ton of opportunities to do other things, things I loved and cared about. By exposing myself to uncomfortable experiences, I've learned that it is possible to accept uncertainty as part of life and stop wasting my time trying to avoid it or control it.

—DANIELA

The fact that it's a totally human experience to have feelings has implications for how we approach mental health. It means we're not going to invest our time and energy in trying to avoid or control thoughts or feelings. We can experience whatever happens in our heads. So the focus of our work to build better mental health and maintain it isn't targeted at symptom relief. Instead, we need to shift the focus to the problems that are interfering with our ability to do what we want to do in life. We need to recognize our problems and not get caught up in the superficial symptoms. That's the second important concept we'll explore.

This is something we understand with physical fitness. Let's say

I'm feeling pain in my knee when I'm running and that persists even when I'm not running. I feel the pain the moment I wake up in the morning. That pain begins to interfere with everyday activities. I can no longer do many of the activities I love doing and associate with my identity. So I'd probably go to a doctor or talk with a more experienced runner. He might give me some tips or, in the case of the doctor, prescribe something to relieve the pain, but I would bet he'd focus on why I'm experiencing that pain. It could be my gait, or how my foot contacts the pavement, or the shoes I'm wearing, or maybe it's because of that time I fractured my ankle in a karate tournament as a teenager but didn't go to the doctor or tell anybody that my foot turned purple. Something I'm doing, or something that's happening, or something that happened to me, led to the experience of that pain. Whatever it is, I need to look past the pain and make changes around the problem(s) leading to that pain if I want to get back to exercising and functioning the way I want to function. I might have to unlearn how I've been running for years. I might have to work with a therapist doing intense, often painful exercises to rehabilitate the knee and learn healthier ways of running.

With physical fitness, that's how we would approach an issue that's interfering with our ability to function in life. We have to do the same with mental health issues.

Pain is a symptom. It might be something I feel, and something I don't want to feel, but focusing all of my energy on escaping the pain won't get rid of the thing causing the pain. In fact, if I try to eliminate the pain, and I succeed, but I continue with everything I was doing before the pain started, it's entirely possible that the cause of the pain will worsen and do lasting damage in my life. This is especially true with mental health challenges.

Not only does relieving the symptoms of mental health issues have the potential to let those issues worsen, but they can worsen to a degree that effectively or literally ends your life. Mental health issues are never benign. They're like a monster chewing on your leg. That's the kind of knee pain we're dealing with here. You could go to the doctor and try to get relief from that pain, but when there's a monster chewing your leg into hamburger meat, don't mistake relief from the pain of the monster's bite for escape from the monster's attack.

Too often, we go searching for relief from feelings we don't like and we find it. Then the monster moves on to chewing another part of us. We go hunting for relief from that pain. Again, we seek out relief. The monster eats another part of us, the pain rises to our attention again, and we find another way to relieve that pain. Eventually, the monster devours us completely.

Anxiety, depression, intrusive thoughts, craving, distress, and all of the other feelings we dislike are types of pain. You can get rid of that pain if you want. There are many ways to do that. You've probably tried most of them. I tried most of them, too. And there are many situations where relief from pain is a key support for doing intense rehabilitation work or empowering us to fight off the monsters chewing up our lives. But we have to go after the source of the pain and make changes there.

If we're experiencing pain from mental health challenges, it can be very difficult to see past that pain and recognize the monster chewing on us. But we have to ask how our leg got into a monster's mouth in the first place, how we can get it out of there, and how we can prevent that from happening again in the future.

I can't tell you exactly what your monsters are. Be curious and look past the pain to see the problems underneath. Sometimes those problems will be outside of your direct control, in contextual factors like inequality or violence—monsters that leap out of the dark and attack you. Quite often, however, the problems will be things that you're doing. For instance, when you engage in compulsions, it's like walking up to a hungry monster and sticking your leg in its mouth. Of course the monster bites you. It's only natural that you experience pain.

WHAT'S A COMPULSION?

I'll be talking about compulsions throughout the book. They are the actions we engage in that make our mental health worse. I define a compulsion as **anything you do to cope with, check on, or control uncertainty, anxiety, and other feelings you don't like.** Understanding this has been the single biggest help with taking care of my mental health. If I engage in coping, checking, and controlling behaviors, I'm choosing to experience more uncertainty, more anxiety, and more of the feelings I don't like at ever-increasing levels of complexity and severity.

With compulsions, look for that pattern of coping, checking, and controlling in reaction to unwanted experiences. Compulsions vary in their superficial characteristics. Some are the more stereotypical, overtly obvious compulsions we might associate with mental health issues, like returning home to check that you unplugged all of the appliances because you're afraid of causing a fire, or getting high every day as an attempt to quiet the thoughts in your head, or shouting at people in the street because you think they're trying to steal your ideas, or sending your partner a deluge of text messages to be certain that she loves you, or pulling out hair to cope with feelings you don't know how to handle, or restricting what you eat as an attempt to control what you think others think about you. But compulsions can be present in any activity, like when we're checking our phones.

That first exercise we did, where you practiced not checking your phone when you got the urge to check it, was about learning the basics of cutting out a compulsion. When you experience uncertainty about a message and you immediately check your phone to make that uncertainty go away, that's a compulsion, in a very simple, everyday, normal form.

Somebody might engage in compulsions by always controlling conversations and manipulating the truth as a way to control fears about being disliked or not valued. That's not something obvious, like engaging in violence to control other people, but the rationale behind it is the same: there's a fear about something that could happen and then there's an attempt to control that fear.

Many compulsions "work" phenomenally well for shorter and shorter periods of time until they don't work at all. They get rid of the immediate pain. But they always cause more pain in the long term. You're not solving anything with compulsions. Your "solutions" are part of the problem. They lead to more pain. You can see this pattern at work any time you procrastinate.

I WAS AN EXPERT PROCRASTINATOR

I was an impressively skilled procrastinator for much of my life. In university I took a Chinese poetry course to fill a degree requirement. This was at a point in my university career when I was playing lots of video games, spending hours online, and I was involved in so many extracurricular activities that I usually neglected those as well. With all of those important things to do, there was no time left for studying. I did schoolwork only when the panicked pressure of failing became so intolerable that I would actually pick up a book.

I fell behind in my classes. That made me anxious. With that increase in anxiety, I spent even more time trying to escape the pressure.

Thinking about the amount of reading that was required for my poetry class felt like I was trying to tickle a panic attack out of my stomach. I held on to the belief that I was so smart I could always pull an all-nighter and study whatever I needed to know for the final exam. I could handle a thousand years of Chinese poetry in a night.

Sheer terror and arrogance are a potent mixture of emotions that accomplish amazing disasters.

In the final weeks of the semester, I went to the last class of Chinese poetry to find out what was on the exam so I could masterfully cram it into my brain. I loved that professors always covered the exam topics in the last class.

I walked into the windowless cinder-block box of a classroom and I remember noticing that the room seemed abnormally full even though there were still several minutes before class started. I sat down to wait for class to start, the professor came in a little while later, and he immediately began handing out exam papers.

This kind professor had offered to do an in-class exam before the normal exam period so that everybody could focus on their exams for other (arguably more important) classes. What a nice professor! Such a diligent class of poetry students! And, oh my God, there was literally no way I could bullshit my way through the exam because I hadn't read any of the poems. I didn't know my Li Yu from my Hanshan. I didn't even know those were things I didn't know.

If I'd read any of the poems for the class, I'm sure I could have recited one at that moment to express precisely how I felt. But because I hadn't, all I was left with was the panicked poetry of my heart thumping at rib cage–busting intensity. The feeling of anxiety in my body had gone from its usual 100 to 100 trillion in a second. My face probably flushed an amazing shade of red. I don't remember what I said to the professor. I think I told him I felt sick, which wasn't exactly a lie at that moment. He agreed to let me leave and write the exam later. Somehow, I passed the course. To that very wonderful professor: 谢谢!

I was very stressed afterward. That was totally natural to experience given the months of compulsions I'd invested in avoiding all of the feelings I didn't like: the difficulty, the boredom, and then later, the anxiety.

Pain is a predictable outcome of those avoidance compulsions. It's very normal to feel pain when a monster bites you. It's very normal to feel more anxiety when you try to avoid things that make you anxious. If you want to run a marathon but you don't feel like training, and you don't start practicing until a few weeks before the marathon when you feel the pressure of that approaching deadline, what will your experience be like when you're running that marathon? Probably painful. The problem, however, is not the marathon or the pain or the exhaustion you feel. The problem was the months of avoiding practice before the marathon. The problem probably felt good. It wasn't distressing. You probably had reasons to put off that practice. It seemed rational.

Had I gone to get help at campus psych services in the week following that stressful exam experience, I might have presented the pain and stress as the problem. I had a panic attack in class! I was stressed about exams! Anxious about my grades! What could I do to get rid of that anxiety? But asking that is like somebody in the midst of a marathon asking how to be less exhausted or feel less pain. I would've been seeking help for a symptom that's only a natural result of months invested in a problem.

BREAK THE COMPULSION ADDICTION

Here's the thing with compulsions: Even though we engage in them as an attempt to cope with, check on, and control experiences we don't like, compulsions become their own problem. As with any addiction, when you start to cut them out, you experience all of the pain from all of the monster bites that you were using them to avoid.

Along with laying out the basic principles of mental health and emotional fitness, the first several chapters of this book focus on helping you to better understand how coping, checking, and controlling as a reaction to uncertainty and other feelings you don't like are actually fueling those experiences. They always cause more of what you're trying to avoid.

In the past, I experienced lots of pain around other people. A lot of that pain had to do with wanting other people not to dislike me. That's something that's very difficult to be certain about because we don't know what other people are thinking and we can't control what they're thinking. So I would do many things that I believed would help prevent my being disliked. For instance, I tried to avoid expressing opinions or likes or dislikes. I quickly discounted whatever I cared about. I liked whatever you liked. I disliked whatever you disliked. We like the same things! We hate the same things! Let's be friends!

My reaction to the pain was to do things that only allowed the problem to worsen. That's a very common reaction. Instead of recognizing the compulsions—like lying to others to try to get them to like me—I spent years focused on the symptoms created by the compulsions: stress, fatigue, fear, anxiety, depression, conflict, loneliness. Being so caught up in the compulsions prevented me from ever getting at the underlying issues I had around other people. I was so hooked on trying to get people to like me, I never addressed my fears about being alone or disliked. So those fears deepened.

Nothing changed until I started eliminating the compulsions. Then I had to address the problems I'd been hiding beneath them.

To help you with clearing out the compulsions so you can begin to get at what's underneath, this chapter's exercise will explore how you're doing what you're doing in your life. You'll also look at what you want to be doing in your life. Clearly articulating those two points will give you your starting point and destination for the journey of building better mental health.

EXERCISE: The Inventories

We're going to do two connected exercises: the Inventory and the Ideal Inventory. They're visual data collection exercises about your life. The Inventory is very simple but powerful. It works like this:

1. Grab a pen and some paper. Make sure it's tangible and relatively permanent. It needs to be something you can pull out later and look at. This is not a step you can do in

your head. You can do this digitally if you want to, but read through the entire exercise first and make sure your digital tools won't restrict you.

2. Write or draw how you spend your time and energy in life. This is not what you want to be true, but what *is* true about you right now, at this point in your life. Show it all.

You might have the urge to censor yourself, but just ignore that little voice in your head. Don't worry about anyone else seeing this—you have complete permission to hide this away in your deepest, darkest sock drawer or burn it when you're through using it. So get the words out of your head.

If you're struggling with alcohol, show how much time and energy gets spent on that struggle. Do you cook all of the time? Write that down. What do you often cook? Do you speak Portuguese at home and English at work? Get it on there. Do you spend a couple of hours every day fantasizing about a colleague and surreptitiously visiting his social media profiles? Show how much of your working hours that takes up. What do you do in the mornings? What do you do in your head all day? How do you interact with other people? How much of your life do you control? Try to capture everything about how you spend your time and energy.

Show relationships between activities. Do some activities happen inside of other activities? When I do this exercise I like to draw blobs—I use their size, proximity to one another, and positioning to express meaning about the different activities. Like this:

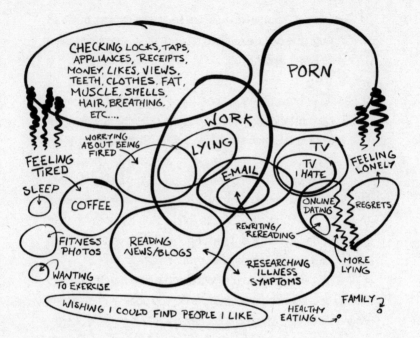

Getting that all out in the open can make you feel nervous. I know I was shaking after the first time I did this. I thought I'd spend about thirty minutes in a coffee shop writing it, and ended up staying there for two intense hours.

That first Inventory is only the beginning. After you've completed your Inventory, it's time for the Ideal Inventory. You'll create that with the same process, but this time, create your Inventory for the future. Imagine a day one year from now and visualize how you want to spend your time and energy on that day. What compulsions have you eliminated from your life so they don't even show up on your Inventory? What healthy activities have you introduced? What activities or people are only a tiny piece of your current Inventory but grow to a more significant portion of your Ideal Inventory?

When I first did my Ideal Inventory, I emphasized many of the activities I often thought about but didn't actually do or even know how to incorporate into my life, like cooking, weight lifting, and meditation. I cut out all of the time I was spending on compulsions. I added in much more time devoted to building social relationships. From doing the Inventory, it was also clear to me that I had the time to spend on doing things I loved, even if it was outside of my work and schedule. My Ideal Inventory was realistic but firmly rooted in my passions.

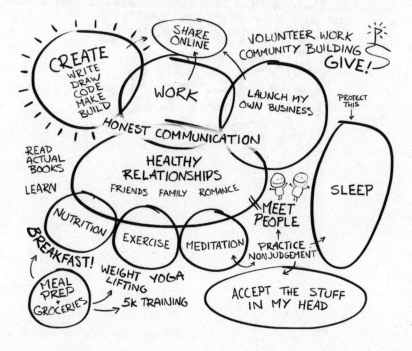

When you've completed both inventories, take some time to reflect on the gap between the two of them. That gap is your journey ahead. All of the skills and concepts we cover in this book will help you take the journey between those two points.

DON'T MISTAKE
RELIEF FROM THE
PAIN OF THE
MONSTER'S BITE
FOR ESCAPE
FROM THE
MONSTER'S
ATTACK

Practice mindfulness

> To understand how to accept the stuff in my head, it helped
> me to see it all as waves in the ocean. I don't choose when a
> thought can just stop, similarly to how I can't choose when
> a wave crashes. . . . But it always does crash, just on its own
> time. Sometimes the waves grow higher. Sometimes the waves
> are smaller. Sometimes waves take longer to crash, and some-
> times they crash right away. What waves pop up and when
> they crash is not something under my control. If I were to jump
> into the ocean and try to stop every wave, I would achieve
> nothing. All that is achieved is wasted energy and frustration.
> Same goes with trying to control the stuff in my head.
>
> —SUZANNE

We've covered two important concepts: (1) we feel things because we're
humans (not rocks) and (2) we need to focus on solving underlying
problems, not superficial symptoms. Now we'll get into a fundamental
practice: mindfulness. You'll see this practice in every exercise we do
to build emotional fitness because we need to be present with our
emotions if we want to learn how to handle our emotions better and
handle more of the emotions we don't like so we can do the things in

life that matter to us. The practice of taking care of our mental health is all about learning to accept the stuff in our heads without judgment as we make decisions in the present that help us be happy and healthy over the long term. Mindfulness is the practice that will help you accept the stuff in your head without judgment. The amazing thing is that when you accept your internal experiences—you're not judging a thought as bad, or a feeling as wrong, or an uncertainty as something that needs resolving—you'll eliminate much of what characterizes any struggle with mental health. If you're challenged by the stuff in your head, mindfulness will be a very useful practice to bring into your life. But, like any practice, it's only useful if you practice.

Dr. Jon Kabat-Zinn, the professor, meditation teacher, and researcher who developed mindfulness-based stress reduction (MBSR), a therapeutic approach to applying mindfulness in clinical settings, gives a working definition of mindfulness that I find very useful: "mindfulness is the awareness that arises through paying attention on purpose in the present moment—non-judgmentally."

I like that definition because it explains mindfulness in a way that makes it accessible at any time. You can pay attention on purpose wherever you are. It's also an action we do nonjudgmentally. As we'll explore later, judgment is the spark that sets off the chain reaction of anxiety, fear, and compulsions with which we so often find ourselves struggling.

That definition also emphasizes the importance of intention. Taking care of your health does not happen by accident. You're responsible and empowered to practice mindfulness. If you don't choose to practice mindfulness, it's not strange if your mind is constantly wandering off. It's not weird if you struggle to pay attention. It's not surprising if your mind is always throwing thoughts at you about things you don't want to think about. Those are all natural consequences of practicing mindlessness.

MINDLESSNESS IS A PRACTICE, TOO

To understand mindfulness better, it can help to explore its opposite: mindlessness. If we flip Kabat-Zinn's definition of mindfulness, we could say that mindlessness means not paying attention in any particular way, unintentionally lost in the past or the future, judging everything.

A morning full of practicing mindlessness might go something like this: You wake up and immediately begin checking messages on your phone while you lie in bed, flipping through news stories looking for something interesting until you feel the pressure of being late push you to get up. Then you tweet on the toilet before going to watch the news and write e-mails while you talk with your partner over breakfast as you have conversations in your head with coworkers you need to meet later that day about a project that's alarmingly behind schedule.

The imaginary conversation with your coworkers continues on your commute to work but turns into an argument because you know Susan from HR can't take any criticism and she'll blame you for everything going wrong even though it's not your fault and you told people at the start of the project that this would happen. Why doesn't anybody listen to you?!

You're oblivious to the drive to your office, snapping out of the argument in your head only to honk at a guy in a sports car who cuts you off. The accident that nearly happened flashes through your head. You know exactly what type of jerk drives a car like that.

When you rush into the office, late for your morning department meeting, your body still feels like it's out on the street, about to get in a fight with that other driver. You can feel the tightness in your chest and the butterflies you always get when you're confronting people. That's mixed in with the buzz of anxiety in the back of your head, reminding you that you've got a report to finish that you promised to send to a client later today.

All of those feelings are only exacerbated by the complete and utter hopelessness that this meeting you're now in could produce anything remotely useful. Your body might be in that meeting, smiling to what people are saying, but in your mind you're compiling a list of all the tasks you need to do to get that report finished.

As soon as the meeting is finished, you rush to the kitchen to grab a coffee so you can try to wake up a bit, before collapsing at your desk. You feel stressed from the morning. The work you've got ahead of you for the day seems daunting. There's so much data to collect and analyze and you find that so tedious.

You flip through your social media accounts for a few minutes. You know you'll feel the urge to check them later so you want to get that out of the way. After thirty minutes, you put on a podcast for some background noise, you open up the report document, and you get started.

At least, you want to get started, but it's difficult to focus. You write a few sentences, and then you're pulling out your phone again without even noticing you've done it, checking your social media accounts again, then your e-mail. There aren't any new messages. You check them all again. Then there is a new message! You respond to that. Then back to the report. It's agonizingly difficult to focus on it. You go online to look for jobs that pay well but won't require much extra schooling. Maybe you should become a software developer? You read an article online recently about how much developers get paid. Software start-up offices have Ping-Pong tables and you would love to play Ping-Pong at work. . . .

PRACTICE GIVES YOU SKILLS

That was mindlessness at work: your mind constantly jumping to a different place and time, judging everything, reacting to those judgments, relying on anxiety about the past and the future to fuel all of your actions, bouncing from one crisis to the next.

If you look at everything in that example leading up to the mome
you wanted to start working on that report, it's not at all surprising
that focusing on work was difficult. The practice of mindlessness, like
any practice, has totally natural consequences: Your brain gets better
at it and wants to do it even more. Brains like to do the things they do
repeatedly. It's easy. It saves energy. After hours of priming your mind
to not be present, it's normal for it to continue functioning that way.
How many hours for how many days have you committed to the
practice of mindlessness?

If we spend all morning practicing distraction, it's not a sign of
illness if we then discover we can't do the things we want to do when
we want to do them. If you have trouble paying attention and your
days are in any way similar to what I described, you don't have an
attention deficit disorder. You can't blame the Internet or smartphones
for being distracting. You have a brain. And your brain is a very good
learner. It's doing exactly what you trained it to do.

I spent years practicing mindlessness. I was very skilled at it. Being
mindless became my default mode in every situation, every day. I
came to rely on that practice as the only way I knew how to
function. I thought that way of living and working was helping me,
but it was a maladaptive skill. I lost control of the monster I'd raised
in my brain.

ALLOCATING BANDWIDTH FOR YOUR SEVEN SENSES

When we talk about extra senses, it's usually about paranormal powers,
but this isn't about seeing ghosts or predicting the future. I assure you
this is totally grounded in a reality you're experiencing. Learning how
to meditate and practice mindfulness in my daily life has helped me to
recognize that I have seven senses. I experience sight, sound, touch,
smell, taste, thought, and emotion.

ur thoughts and emotions. They are not you. You
like a shout in the street, the sting of a wasp, a
the reek of decay, the most delicious dessert melting
tongue.

When we approach thoughts and emotions as senses, as experiences we can be aware of, it opens up the opportunity to move awareness around our different senses. This is an especially useful skill to cultivate if you're obsessively focused on thoughts spinning in your head or you're overwhelmed by emotions.

You've probably had an experience when you were reading intently and didn't hear somebody call your name, or you were so engrossed in the movie you were watching that you forgot about the pain that kept you home from school that day, or you noticed that staying constantly busy around other people seemed to shut out all of the intrusive thoughts that bother you when you're alone. That's selective attention. We can't process all of the information coming through from our senses at any given moment. Our awareness has a fixed amount of bandwidth for our senses. If we allocate all of the bandwidth to one or only a few senses, there's no space for the others.

You can experiment with this right now: Notice what your butt is in contact with. Be aware of that physical contact with whatever you're sitting or lying on right now. Or if you're standing crammed on public transit right now, notice the part of your body touching the person next to you. Awareness of that physical contact probably wasn't there a moment ago. You were reading or listening. Your awareness was concentrated on sight and thought. But the physical contact was there. You simply weren't allocating any of your awareness bandwidth to that experience.

This ability to allocate bandwidth to your various senses is an ability you can develop and practice. It's an ability you've been constantly practicing, every day, even if you weren't aware of it.

When we're struggling with the stuff in our heads, we give all of that awareness bandwidth to those thoughts and emotions we want to avoid or control. That's a practice. We get skilled at it. There's only a tiny bit of bandwidth left over for processing the world around us and we become increasingly less skilled at that. So it becomes easier to ruminate about what we think our partner might have said than hearing what she actually said. A memory from the past about an event that *didn't* happen can create more anxiety than something that *is* happening. The stuff in our heads becomes more real and meaningful than reality. Eventually it becomes a filter through which we experience our other senses, to such an extent that we experience only the filter. We get stuck bludgeoning every experience with the same distorted judgments, smothering everything with anxiety or mania or depression. The practice of mindfulness will give you the skills to flexibly choose how you allocate awareness to your experiences.

DOING WHAT YOU'RE DOING, BEING WHERE YOU'RE BEING

Mindfulness isn't an activity separate from our everyday lives. It's a way of doing and being. You don't need extra time in your life to practice mindfulness. In fact, you'll find it gives you more time because you'll actually be present for the life you're living. With mindlessness, you get stuck living a life that either won't happen or you wish didn't happen. When you're caught up in the practice of mindlessness, death becomes very frightening because you're acutely aware of moving closer and closer to the end of the life you could've had. Mindfulness is an opportunity to live.

To practice mindfulness, you simply keep your mind and body in the same place, doing what you're doing, being where you're being. If you're eating, eat. If you're listening, listen. If you're giving, give. If you're walking, walk. If you're shitting, shit. If you're driving, drive. If you're fucking, fuck. If you're singing, sing. If you're cooking, cook. If you're washing, wash.

We can find incredible enjoyment in the present moment when we're present to experience that enjoyment, doing whatever we're doing.

BUT WON'T MINDFULNESS SLOW ME DOWN? I HAVE THINGS TO DO!

The practice of mindfulness might sound like it won't fit into your hectic life. It might seem like you're being asked to give up the time you spend solving problems in your head, preparing for conversations, and coming up with all of your best ideas. How can anybody accomplish anything if they're not on their phone texting their partner while eating their lunch and writing an e-mail to their boss at the same time that they're working on next year's budget spreadsheet and responding to notifications from their social media accounts? Life is designed for twelve hands and three heads, but we have only one brain, so that brain needs to do more. If you can't send important e-mails from your toilet at two a.m., you'll get left behind.

The reality is that practicing mindfulness will help you get more done. I've found it most useful because practicing mindfulness means I'm not constantly catastrophizing about the future or obsessing about how I can change the past. When I struggled with my mental health, my brain was constantly spinning this aggressively anxious hamster of thoughts, which made me only even more anxious and miserable. I was stressed all of the time by my own doing. I had to give up so much energy just to deal with how upset I was constantly making myself. Now that I don't do that anymore, I have much more energy to put into doing what I actually care about.

Confirmation bias makes it easy for us to remember the great ideas we came up with while being totally distracted from doing something else. We can easily forget all of the times we made ourselves miserable and anxious and upset ruminating about something in the past or the future while our bodies were left to run on autopilot in the present.

EXERCISE: Everyday Mindfulness

Mindfulness is something you can practice every day. You have the opportunity, in any moment, to be present. You can feel what you're feeling and experience what you're experiencing as you do what you're doing. Practice within the context in which you live. I'll share some different situations in which you can try practicing mindfulness to explore it more deeply:

Mindful Mobility

Whether you walk, use a wheelchair, run, bike, drive, fly, or move by any other means, try practicing mindfulness while you do it.

Of all the activities I now do to maintain my mental health, mindful walking is one that I enjoy immensely. I didn't know it was possible to walk without constantly spinning the hamster wheel of thoughts in my head.

In the past, I intentionally approached walking as time to obsess, to stay inside my head and shut out my other senses. I wouldn't see or hear anything around me because I was too busy debating in my head with politicians I disagreed with, or trying to explain to an ex why it was her fault we broke up, or digging in my memories for evidence that would prove I hadn't committed a crime or done something mean to a friend.

When I wasn't focused inward, I'd let my brain run all over the world around me, like a deranged, untrained puppy, sniffing and judging and pissing on everything.

Moving through the world mindfully is about being present to your current experience. It's about keeping that rambunctious puppy brain beside you, not running off to the past or the future. It's about being aware of the world and the experience you're having in it.

Notice how judgments pop into your head. Can you recognize those judgments but not chase after them? Try moving your awareness around your senses. Instead of allocating attention to thoughts or judgments, can you practice giving more bandwidth to awareness of sounds? Or what you see? Or the movement of your body in the present moment?

There is incredible enjoyment to discover in moving through the world mindfully, whether you're going out on a hot date or to the most important business meeting of your life or to the store to buy toilet paper.

Mindful Listening

Today or sometime in the week ahead, try entering into a conversation with the intention of practicing mindful listening. Be there with the person or people with whom you're having the conversation. When you notice yourself chasing after thoughts and you've started to worry about whether there's something in your teeth, or what you should say next so people think you're smart and funny, or if there's somebody more interesting you could be talking to, simply bring your awareness back to the present. Listen. Listen to what they say without attaching judgments and extra baggage to their words. Give understanding instead of trying to get it. Can you bring enjoyment to simply listening instead of approaching each conversation like a danger to avoid or a test you need to ace?

As you begin this practice, it might only be about noticing how much stuff you're doing in your head. It might be very difficult to stop doing all of that stuff and simply listen. That's okay. Be aware of the difficulty. You don't have to judge yourself for it. You've probably invested years in getting skilled at mindless listening.

Mindful Seeing

This one might be excruciatingly difficult: try to see something without doing a million other things, outside or inside your head.

Go to a beautiful spot and see the beauty. No selfies. Notice when you get lost in thoughts. Bring your awareness back to what you see.

Try watching a TV show or a movie and doing only that. Not watching it while doing homework. Not watching it with your phone in one hand and a burrito in the other. Not watching it while planning e-mails you'll write as soon as it's done. Can you watch it completely without skipping ahead or turning the channel or searching for something better? Can you practice not judging the people you're watching?

Mindful Cooking

This one might be my favorite: Prepare a meal mindfully. You don't need to put music on or listen to a podcast as you cook. Try to open up all of your senses to the meal you're preparing. Enjoy the food. Recognize all of the work that went into getting it to you. Water and sunshine and the energy of so many people made that food possible. Enjoy that you're preparing that food for yourself or for others. Recognize the work you're doing for you.

If you don't know how to cook, that's okay. I didn't, either. I had many compulsions in the kitchen, so cooking was not something I delved into when I struggled with my mental health. But as I took steps to getting over mental illness, I saw that I needed to do a lot of work in the kitchen to help my brain. So I took cooking classes. The classes created opportunities to tackle fears I had about knives, food poisoning, stoves, and being a terrible chef. By learning how to handle and prepare food as I overcame those fears, cooking also became a way to practice mindfulness. Now the act of cooking each day is a way I can nourish my body while also practicing the skills that help me take care of my mental health.

HOW TO SUCCEED AT MINDFULNESS:

1. DO THE THING YOU'RE DOING

2. BREATHE

3. KEEP DOING THE FIRST TWO STEPS

Meditate

If life were an orchestra and mindfulness were music, meditation would be a practice drill with your instrument that would improve your capacity to play music. Meditation is the focused practice of mindfulness skills. When you start to meditate regularly, it will feel like developing strength and endurance in your head that you can then apply through mindfulness in your everyday life. If you notice yourself struggling to apply mindfulness in specific experiences, meditation provides an opportunity to work on your skills to address those challenges. That's why I've divided mindfulness and meditation into two different steps.

Like any kind of drill to develop a skill, meditation is difficult. You may struggle with it (a lot). Meditation is not a magical panacea that brings instant calm and tranquillity, washing away anxiety and every other emotion you don't like. Meditation is a practice, not a light switch. And it's a practice you need to begin incorporating into your life. It'll take time to make space for it, so get started. I've included it at this point in the book because it's not something to do after you get your mental health and emotions sorted out. Start now, even if it's a struggle.

If you don't meditate, meditation is very difficult and you won't experience any of its benefits. If you don't practice meditation, it's completely natural to struggle with paying attention, to have difficulty handling emotions, or to be incapable of stopping that hamster wheel of thoughts spinning in your head.

If you do meditate, meditation is still difficult and you might experience some benefits eventually. So enjoy the practice of meditation for itself, not for some distant outcome you're craving. Treat it like a friend. Don't bring it into your life only to take from it. If you're selfish with meditation, you will have an unhappy relationship with it.

With practicing meditation or any skill we explore in this book, you can come to enjoy the challenge of bringing it into your life. I hope you can discover that the challenges of meditation are also benefits of the practice. They'll bind your relationship with it.

MEDITATION IS A HUMAN PRACTICE

Meditation is the oldest new thing. Religions around the world have played an important role in carrying this practice from ancient times into our contemporary era. When I became interested in meditation and wanted to learn more about it, the only groups I could find in my city were all connected to religions. For some of these groups, calling them religions was a very liberal use of the word. They were cults. But they had FREE meditation classes (with juice and COOKIES)!

So I would go to a session and there'd be all of this singing and chanting and reading passages from religious books tacked onto the meditation. And the cookies were never delicious cookies. Nobody feels closer to enlightenment when they're eating nasty cookies. It took me a long time to find a meditation group that I liked.

The connection to religion can be a barrier for many people when they try to access the benefits of meditation. You might hear about research showing that meditating for eight weeks can increase gray matter density in areas of your brain associated with memory and learning, or that long-term meditators exhibit more gray matter in areas associated with sensory awareness and executive decision making when compared with people who don't meditate, or that it supports people in being less emotionally triggered, or that it helps you keep your mind from wandering off when writing tests, and you might think: "Wow, I want to get me some of that!" But then you find the closest meditation group and the guy at the front of the room starts talking about having three eyes and past lives and aligning his chakras and you quickly line up your chakras straight out the door.

Meditation is a fundamentally human practice. You sit there, you breathe, you be. It's a focused, intentional practice of being mindful of being. It strips away everything except existence. It's as human as you can get.

Religion can be part of that or not. When I'm talking about meditation or mindfulness throughout this book, I'm talking about them as actions that anybody can practice. Religion need not be attached to the exercise of meditation any more than it needs to be attached to any other exercise.

There's a chapter coming up later on nonjudgment, and if you feel an urge to dismiss meditation simply because it has been associated with religion or a religion that you don't practice, then I'd suggest you get a head start on practicing nonjudgment. My judgments were a barrier to getting started with meditation at first. The group I attend at the moment is led by a teacher, Ronit Jinich, who practices in the tradition of the Zen teacher Thich Nhat Hanh. There are certainly many aspects of the practice that are Buddhist, but I am not Buddhist, nor do I need to be to find value in stopping, sitting, and breathing with my neighbors. I sometimes make cookies to bring to class.

I STRUGGLE WITH MEDITATION

That struggle is useful. It helps me learn how to meditate. My unruly puppy mind constantly wants to run around, chase after every stick my brain throws at it, and find inappropriate places to stick its nose. Even when my brain does come back to me in the present, it's usually dragging something dead and disgusting it dug up from the past.

Learning how to get my mind to sit and breathe with me has been a long and useful journey. From years of training, my mind has learned to always be running off into the past or the future. Finding time for meditation is also challenging amid all of the competing priorities in my life. I'm sure you also have a long list of things you could be doing at any moment, and that list is always growing longer. I hope you learn the benefits of prioritizing meditation on that list. It's not something I can convince you to prioritize. If you don't run, it must seem absurd to see people waking up early to go jogging in the cold morning air. If you haven't experienced the benefits of that practice, it's impossible to imagine why somebody would prioritize that. Let's talk more about running as a way to help you get your meditation practice going.

CONSIDER HOW YOU WOULD BECOME A RUNNER

Starting a meditation practice is analogous to starting a running practice. They parallel each other to an uncanny extent, in skills and in outcomes. On top of that, whether you visit a meditation group or a running group, at the end of the session you're guaranteed there'll always be people whining about their knees.

If somebody wanted to start running, she would start small, she'd do it with a partner or join a group or get a coach, she'd make time in her life for it, she'd do it consistently if she wanted to see results, she'd make changes throughout her life to support running, and so on. This is all true with meditation as well: no one can persuade you to do it; you have to want to practice and make time for it. Using running as an analogue, consider the following as you start your meditation practice:

1. **Start small.**

    If you haven't been meditating regularly (or at all), it's totally natural to not have the skills or capacity to meditate for very long. Start with ten or fifteen minutes each day for the first week. Even if you've meditated in the past but you've taken a break for many months, you'll find it's difficult again, just as you would find running difficult if you took a break from that for several months.

2. **Stay consistent.**

    The ability to pay attention is exactly like your capacity for cardiovascular endurance. If you're not consistently using it and improving it, then it's getting worse. If you run a 5K race but then stop training right after, how long before you wouldn't be able to run a 5K without stopping? Not very long. So plan for the long term with meditation. It has to become part of your life. Consider how you've made other practices consistent parts of your life—even unhealthy practices. What makes them stick?

3. **Push into the discomfort while acknowledging your limits.**

    Start small but challenge yourself. It's okay to struggle with meditation. Find where it's difficult and give yourself permission to struggle. You'll discover where your limits are. Gradually push into them. It might be useful to start with guided meditation audio tracks because it gives you something extra to focus on. I'd suggest searching online for Jon Kabat-Zinn's recordings for the Mindfulness-Based Stress Reduction course. Many people I work with enjoy Andy Puddicombe's work and his Headspace app. For loving-kindness meditation, which we'll talk about later in this book, Sharon Salzberg has many recordings and Ronit Jinich also has some useful audio guides online that help break down the steps of practicing loving-kindness meditation. We'll explore more later about why it's so tough to practice loving yourself. Also try meditating without an audio guide. What challenges arise? How does your mind behave differently? What happens when you sit for a much longer period of time?

4. Be kind to yourself. Why would you be able to meditate?

You might suck at meditation. Unless there's a special reason you shouldn't suck at it, expect to suck at it. That's wonderful! You're on an exciting journey with this practice. If you want to judge yourself or get angry at meditation for not "working," you can do that, but adding that extra baggage will make this experience only more difficult. How will you enjoy sitting and breathing with your brain if you're also hauling around heavy judgments and big assumptions? Would you expect yourself to run a marathon a month after you picked up running as a hobby?

5. Expect the unexpected.

If you were new to running, you'd experience aches and pains and pleasurable sensations and all sorts of fascinating side effects. Shin splints? Higher libido? Who knows what might happen?! You've never used your body like that before, and if you're new to meditation, you've never used your mind like this before. Whatever experiences you have will be awesome experiences to have while meditating. You can be mindful of those emotions, thoughts, or physical sensations. That *is* the practice. Invite them to sit beside you while you breathe. Let them pile on top of you. Let them run away on their own. You don't have to judge them or yourself for experiencing them. You don't have to get rid of them. Can you be willing to let them be?

6. **Make time.**

I don't meditate at the same time every day. I also don't exercise at the same time every day. My schedule is constantly changing. What's important is that I schedule time to meditate. In the morning, I figure out a time to meditate and then I defend that time. It would be easy to think of a million reasons why I'm too busy today and can always meditate for extra time tomorrow to make up for it. But that meeting with my breath is something I respect as I would any other meeting. I can't reschedule a meeting with such an important partner. It might be the most important meeting I have all day.

7. **Explore the practice.**

One of the benefits to adopting such an ancient practice is that you can support yourself with an immense array of books, videos, audio tracks, apps, scrolls, and even stone tablets. You don't have to meditate in a vacuum. Explore different types of meditation. Read about meditation in books written by people who died centuries ago. Any challenge that you run into is a challenge that somebody else has already written about. Dive into that wealth of wisdom.

8. **Connect with other people.**

A great way to support your meditation practice is to connect with others. It's like joining a running group—it can help with consistency and overcoming challenges along the way. You don't even need to do it in person if there's no group in your area. Connect with people online who share similar meditation goals and practices. Having meditation buddies can help to remind you to meditate and you can discuss how to overcome challenges together.

9. **Modify your practice to fit your context.**

People run in different ways. Some like trail running, others like obstacle races, others hit the treadmill at the gym, some run as part of triathlons, others ditch running in favor of skiing or swimming or racing wheelchairs. Common among all of them is that they build endurance and strength by pushing into their limits. There are many types of meditation. Explore what works for you. Try not to get caught up in the superficial characteristics of meditation. If you can't sit cross-legged on the floor, don't. Find a way to practice that's comfortable for you within your context.

10. **Set goals that rocks can't do better than you.**

As with anything related to mental health, don't forget this. I find it useful to set goals that are entirely in my control. I control how much I meditate each day. That's about it. I don't control what pops into my head or what happens around me while I meditate. I don't control any feelings I might have while I meditate. I don't control any long-term outcomes of meditating. I control only paying attention to my next breath. How much will you meditate each day?

BUT WHAT IF I TRIED MEDITATION AND IT DIDN'T WORK?

Telling somebody that you tried meditation and it didn't work is like telling somebody that you tried cooking and it didn't work. Either you were trying to get something it doesn't provide, you haven't practiced it consistently for long enough, you were putting lots of effort into skills that make things worse, or you were doing some combination of those. If all you do is burn things, change how you do things.

Meditation works. It's very easy to get it to work for you. When you meditate, you've successfully reached the goal of meditation. You're successful at it if you're doing it. There's nothing else to pursue.

When people encounter barriers with meditation, they're typically struggling with the concepts we covered at the beginning of the book: not approaching mental health and emotional fitness as practices, trying to be like a rock that doesn't feel or think, and trying to relieve symptoms instead of tackling problems. Let's look at how the concepts from the previous chapters apply in your meditation practice:

Barrier #1: Not approaching mental health and emotional fitness as practices

With any practice, whether it's cooking, performing music, running, or learning how to handle the stuff in your head, you push into difficult experiences and learn new skills to keep going. Through regular practice, your endurance, flexibility, precision, strength, and competency improve. Emotional fitness isn't something you can directly change, in the same way that you can't flip a switch and instantly learn how to play an instrument or have the capacity to run a marathon. Improvement at anything is an outcome of consistent practice. Meditation is a practice that can help you push into your limits. When you sit or lie down to breathe in the present, you'll experience feelings, thoughts, and physical sensations you don't like. That will give you the opportunity to build your capacity to handle them. Initially, it's highly likely that will be frustrating. Thoughts will pop up about something stupid you said yesterday, or you'll feel overwhelmed by physical sensations, or you'll automatically begin reassuring yourself that you're not a stupid, horrible person. You'll have arguments with your ex-boyfriends and current girlfriends. You'll get flooded with emotions you've been covering up. You might spend the entire time worrying about work and then get angry at yourself for "wasting" your meditation time and being "bad" at it. All of this is normal. Having stuff in your head, whatever that stuff is, is totally normal. Chasing after it is normal. That's why we start to practice meditation, so we can learn how to bring our awareness back to the present.

Practice is the purpose. That's what we're there to do. We notice when we start chasing after thoughts and judgments and then we bring our awareness back to the present. It's an exercise, like jogging one foot after the other on the pavement, practicing scales on the piano, or working through math equations in a textbook. And we'll reach our limits, again and again. We won't be able to go any further or sit any longer or apply a specific technique. So we try again.

Barrier #2: Trying not to feel or think

If you go to a bookstore with many meditation or mindfulness-based therapy books, I bet the dominant graphic design motif you would see on those book covers would be rocks. There would be pictures of smooth rocks stacked on top of one another, or maybe a single rock surrounded by gracefully ridged sand in a Zen garden. But this rock motif is misleading. The purpose of meditation is not to become a rock.

If you come to meditation in the hope that it'll help you escape feelings or thoughts you don't like and you can become an unfeeling rock, then meditation will become only another compulsion. It will bring only more of those unwanted feelings and experiences into your life. With meditation, we can learn how to feel completely. We can experience any thought or emotion without judgment, and explore what it means to have that experience. If you're anxious and you meditate, you'll feel anxious while you meditate. If you struggle with intrusive thoughts, you'll have them when you meditate. That's fine. That's what you're experiencing in the present. Can you become curious about those experiences? Can you welcome them to sit beside you while you meditate? Can you recognize that they're not you, they're experiences?

Barrier #3: Trying to relieve symptoms instead of tackling problems

Meditation is not a replacement for cutting out compulsions, changing unhelpful beliefs, or changing the systems around you that are causing you distress. If you picked up meditation because you wanted to relieve painful symptoms of that monster chewing on you, then you're right back in that example I talked about earlier of the person chasing relief from pain while the monster eats her alive. Meditation isn't something you tack onto an unhealthy life and expect to magically transform that life. Meditation is not a quick fix to problems in your life. It is also not a long fix to problems in your life.

Meditation helps you practice skills and build capacity to accept the stuff in your head while making healthy decisions in the present. It can help you practice handling internal experiences you don't like so you improve your ability to make changes in your life, but you still have to make those changes, whether they're in things you're doing or with things happening to you. If you start meditating because you're stressed at work, either because you work in an unhealthy environment or you're engaging in behaviors at work that make it very stressful for you, don't expect meditation to change that. You'll be a person who works in an unhealthy environment and also meditates. Or you'll be a person who procrastinates all of the time and also happens to meditate (if you don't procrastinate on that as well). So make changes. Practice meditation to build your capacity to make those changes.

*

Now you can put all of this together simply by trying meditation. Whatever happens, happens. The exercise I'll share here is a very basic practice that will help you begin to explore the fundamentals of meditation. You might have an opportunity to experience some of the barriers we just discussed. Later meditation exercises in the book will build on this basic exercise, so be sure to try it out a couple of times if you're new to meditation.

EXERCISE: Meditation

Even with ten minutes of sitting and breathing, you can practice that fundamental skill of having an experience and making a choice aligned with your values.

For this basic exercise, you're going to sit, close your eyes, and practice bringing your awareness to your breath for about ten minutes. If you're listening to the audio version of this book while you're driving or jogging, please don't close your eyes. Keep driving or jogging (with your eyes open). You can try this practice later when you're not moving.

1. Set a timer for ten minutes.

2. Grab a seat and get comfortable.

3. When you're ready, hit START on the timer.

4. Close your eyes and bring your awareness to where you're in contact with whatever it is you're sitting on. Use that awareness of physical contact as an anchor to pin down your chattering mind for a moment. Stay with that sensation for several breaths.

5. When you feel ready, guide your awareness up your body. Take a couple of breaths at each body part and say hello to it. Smile at a knee, wave to your belly button. Be aware of what each body part feels like. Bring your awareness up to your chest as it moves in and out with each breath.

6. Breathe normally. You're simply bringing your awareness to your breath. Follow it as it fills your lungs, and notice the pause, and then follow it all of the way out.

7. Spend some time like this, simply aware of being and breathing. Slow down. Get your brain to sit with you. Keep your awareness with each inhale and each exhale.

8. While you're doing this, you might find that it helps you to focus on your breath if you count each inhale and each exhale. You breathe in: that's one. You breathe out: that's two. In again: one. Out again: two. This isn't about winning a counting competition. Be aware of a breath in and aware of a breath out. Repeat.

9. Your brain will throw some thoughts at you and you might notice that you start to chase after them. That's okay. Bring your awareness back to your breath without judging yourself. This is what meditating is all about: noticing when our awareness has wandered off and then bringing it back. It's like flexing a muscle. That's all we're doing for ten minutes.

10. When the timer goes off, gradually bring your awareness back to the room around you. Notice the sound of the timer. Notice your posture. Come back to that physical experience of touch where you began. And then turn off the timer.

Here's something to consider: When I first began to practice meditation, my thoughts would race incredibly quickly, like the hamster wheel up in my head was being spun by a hamster on steroids. It could take me ten minutes simply to quiet my mind. This exercise might be similarly difficult for you. It may seem like ten minutes of struggle. That's normal. Keep practicing AND try meditating for longer. Those first ten minutes can be like warming up to run—at first your legs are stiff and sore and it won't feel like a good day to exercise. But it is a good day to exercise! Your brain just doesn't know it yet.

Follow your values

One of the things that helped me a lot with my mental health was the decision I made that I prefer spending my time doing the things I love rather than spending it trying to figure out what thoughts are part of my mental health challenges. I just let them come and go, while I live my life the way I want to live it.

—DIANA

Before we get into the chapters about cutting out compulsions that fuel poor mental health, we need to talk about values. We'll come back to values constantly throughout the rest of the book. We build better mental health on our values. Values are the directions we want to move in with each step we take in our lives. Through the Inventory exercises we covered earlier, you can see your values in your Ideal Inventory and recognize how your actions are misaligned with your values when you see things on the Inventory that you're not happy about.

Values are more high level than goals. Goals tell you what you want but values tell you *why* you want them. For example, you might value friendship. With a value like that, you can ask yourself: "How do I build friendships?" You might decide to build them by creating opportunities in your hectic schedule to see your friends and support them. That awareness could translate into a specific goal, like: "I'll organize a time to hang out with my friends at least once every week."

Use your values as a compass on the journey ahead. They'll help you understand which direction to move in when you encounter uncertainty. Once you understand the direction to move in, you can set goals that align with that direction and then you can take action.

The importance of values is something I learned while I was starting therapy and cutting out compulsions, but I didn't actually learn it during therapy sessions, I learned it in the tech sector.

Exposure and response prevention therapy basically involves cutting out the compulsions you would normally engage in when anxious. I'd practiced trying to avoid anxiety my entire life, so my compulsions had become automatic reflexes. It took me more than a week of sweating through excuses and anxious failures before I succeeded for the first time at not checking the front door lock after locking it on my way out. And that was only the initial compulsion I tried to tackle. I had so many others to cut out. At the same time, however, as I was doing exposure and response prevention therapy, I

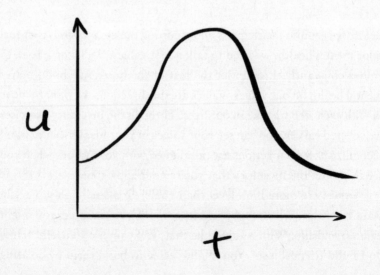

also happened to be in grad school, and had the opportunity to collaborate with Tom Wujec. Tom is a designer and an author, he's given several popular TED talks, he's an Autodesk Fellow, and he facilitates visual thinking workshops to help organizations innovate and find clarity in complex situations. Often, near the start of a workshop, Tom would draw a diagram like this:

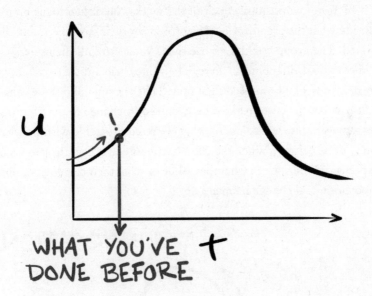

That's the Unhappiness Curve. The *T* is for time and the *U* is for unhappiness. When any person or group innovates—attempting to do something new—they start up the Unhappiness Curve. They experience a drastic increase in feelings they don't like. Uncertainty begins to rise, people worry about what will happen, they're afraid they might lose their jobs, the company will fail, they'll get blamed, etc. The pressure increases to fall back on what they've done before, what's safe, what they know. If they give in to that pressure, they drop down off the curve and go back to what they were doing before. Unhappiness goes away but they also don't innovate. The change they wanted to create doesn't happen. They make a short-term decision to relieve anxiety at the long-term expense of the health and well-being of the organization.

I realized that's what I was doing every time I tried to cut out a compulsion but failed at it. I would experience more and more feelings I didn't like, I'd fall back on what I'd done before, and I'd get temporary relief. But my company was failing. I was not meeting the needs of my number one customer: me.

In Tom's workshops, much of the work would then focus on exploring what the organization, the project, or their customers actually valued. The group could then use those values to pull themselves up and over the Unhappiness Curve. The values help a team say: "Okay, we're all upset and confused right now. That's normal. But these values reflect what our customers want. We need to change to do what our customers want, regardless of what we're comfortable with or what we've done before." When the team members can accept their internal experiences and stick to what they value or what their customers value, innovation and change happens.

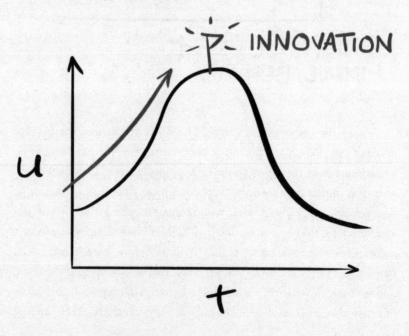

For you, that means accepting that you're anxious or scared, but instead of reacting to it with a decision aimed at short-term relief, you push through that feeling and do what's best and healthiest for the long term.

Although the process for cutting out a compulsion is simple to explain—you accept the stuff in your head and do something you value instead of reacting to it with coping, checking, or controlling compulsions—the practice is much more challenging. Values will help pull you through.

When you're surrounded by uncertainty, values empower you to take a step that contributes to being healthy and happy over the long term. Your values empower you to say things like "Okay, I'm experiencing the urge to go through my partner's social media channels right now to see if he's chatting with anybody who's better looking than me, but what I'll do is put my phone down and make myself breakfast because I value taking care of my health. I don't value investing my time and energy in making myself miserable, jealous, and paranoid."

Because so much of the struggle with our mental health is about trying to avoid uncertainty and move away from experiences, it's normal for that struggle to send us way off course in life. Fear becomes the fuel for our actions. And then our actions are all about things we don't care about. If you give up control of your life to fear and you're not doing things you care about, it's totally normal to sink deep into depression and anxiety. You're being somebody you never wanted to be.

Values are what matter to you. Struggling with mental health is all about pouring your time and energy into things that *don't* matter to you. Building better mental health is all about investing your time and energy in things that *do* matter to you.

DRIVING DANGEROUSLY AWAY FROM FEAR

I grew up in the countryside of southern Ontario, Canada. It's all fields and forests and small towns. Hockey is popular. Ginseng farms have been replacing the old tobacco farms. The sunsets are astounding. The night sky is plastered with stars.

My family lived in a house that was equidistant between two small towns, Norwich and Burford. I went to high school in Burford but also had some friends in Norwich. One year, some of my friends from Norwich invited me to attend their prom, the big end-of-year formal dance at their high school. I was a replacement date for a friend of a friend, so this wasn't a big date with my high school sweetheart. This was only about having a good time.

I went to a friend's place in Norwich before it was time to meet the larger group and head to the dance. At some point, while we were waiting at his house, I realized I didn't have my suit jacket with me. I immediately became nauseated. I knew there would be pictures and I was terrified of being the only guy in the pictures not wearing a suit jacket. People would judge me. I'd be the weird guy who didn't know how to dress properly.

I had to get that suit jacket. But my home was a fifteen-minute drive away, and then I'd have to drive another fifteen minutes more to get back to Norwich. I didn't want to be late for meeting everybody. What would people think if I made the entire group late? I decided my only option was to drive back and get the jacket. And if I had to make the trip, there was only one variable I could control: speed.

I drove way above the speed limit the entire way. It was a straight road—a relatively major road in the area—but with some hills. Had a person been on the other side of one of those hills as I flew over them, I'd have had no chance of stopping before hitting her. I was driving faster than I'd ever driven before. I was speeding so fast and was so oblivious to my surroundings that I didn't notice my father's car, just outside of Norwich, driving in the opposite direction to bring me my suit jacket (cell phones were still rare then). He turned around to follow me but I was going so fast that he caught up to me only when I was a minute away from our house and I slowed down for a turn.

That race to get a jacket haunted me for many years. As I dug the mental illness hole deeper, my anxiety about driving increased. Memories of that drive would leap into my consciousness at random moments and it was like I was right back there. I'd feel the anxiety and adrenaline again. The fact that I could have hit somebody or I could have gotten in an accident made it seem like I *had* gotten in an accident. What if I actually had hit a little kid playing in the ditch by the side of the road and I'd kept on driving without noticing? Maybe the parents discovered what had happened an hour or two later, when their child didn't come home for dinner. I knew I hadn't been paying attention on the race home. For years I was certain there was an ongoing police manhunt out to get me. Every time that memory popped into my head, my stomach was devoured by a gang of vicious moths.

I no longer struggle with anxiety about driving or intrusive thoughts about accidentally killing people or getting arrested—and in the chapters coming up we'll explore what was involved with getting over those obsessions—but now when I look back on the experience, it's a useful reminder of why values are important and how making decisions based on fear can take us away from who we are.

Let's assume that I did hit a kid. The Ministry of Transportation might count it as a traffic accident or a road fatality involving a pedestrian, but was it accidental? I chose to be on that road, driving the way I was driving. I didn't mean to kill somebody, but I didn't mean to drive well or safely. I wanted only to get home as quickly as possible to avoid my fear of being judged for what I was (not) wearing.

Were my actions at that time aligned with what I valued in life? Was attending school dances a life goal of mine? Not at all. Did I love suit jackets? Nope. I was driving like that because I didn't want to feel embarrassed. I was trying to prevent that fear from coming true. But if you'd asked me that day what I cared about in life, would I have said my goal in life was to avoid embarrassment? No.

How cheap am I that I would throw myself away for a fear?

In so many ways, this happens constantly in our lives. We want to be in loving relationships but push people away because our time and energy are pumped into chasing titles and trophies to avoid feeling worthless. We want to be healthy but then stay up all night making ourselves exhausted while we research illness symptoms because we're afraid we're about to die. We want to spend our working hours helping others but our fears about money keep us locked into jobs we hate, making excuses for why the harm we cause others is a necessary evil. We want to enjoy hobbies we're passionate about but instead spend our free time chasing addictions to control feelings we haven't learned to handle.

Are you in charge of how you spend your time and energy in each moment of the day? Or is fear in charge? Because if fear is in charge, it's going to take you to that place you never wanted to be, doing things you never wanted to do. When we put values in charge of our actions, we can move toward the places we've always wanted to go and do the things we've always wanted to do.

WHAT MATTERS TO YOU?

In the previous chapters, we went over skills (like mindfulness) and concepts (like the fact that you are not a rock) to help you practice accepting internal experiences. Once you're practicing acceptance, acting according to your values is the movement that completes this healthy exercise. Acting according to your values is what you'll choose instead of coping, checking, and controlling compulsions. That's the practice of being yourself.

An experience that initially got me thinking I might be struggling with my mental health was noticing I couldn't do the things that mattered to me anymore. There was this gap between who I knew I was and who I was acting as.

I had moved to a new city, and with some money I'd saved up, I decided to take some time to write a novel. It's what I'd always said I wanted to do. Now I had the ideal opportunity to do it. I spent about six months trying to write that book. I got nowhere because I was spending more and more time on compulsions. There were so many anxieties and feelings and uncertainties to react to. I didn't have time for writing.

You might notice a similar tension in your life, between who you know you are and who you're acting as. It's incredibly exhausting to be more than one person. Sometimes we're acting as many different people in different areas of our lives. It's only natural that trying to be somebody you're not creates anxiety and depression.

Mental health is the practice of being yourself. Improving your emotional fitness enables that practice so you can feel whatever you feel while being yourself. That can be frightening sometimes. You might get rejected. You might make somebody angry. You might make many people reject you angrily. But if you're acting as yourself, you can handle whatever happens. There is strength in aligning your identity and your actions. If you pretend to be somebody you're not, and you need to maintain two selves, then those two selves can only ever be half as strong as the single, aligned self. Although they'll likely be much weaker because of all the energy you'll waste running back and forth between your different selves, trying to remember all of the lies you need to maintain, dealing with the frustration of becoming incredibly skilled at being somebody you're not.

If somebody looked at how you currently spend your time and energy and defined you based on that, would you be happy with his definition of you?

When you looked at the results of the Inventory exercise, did you see yourself? Or did you see a whole lot of time and energy being spent on somebody you never wanted to be? What do you need to value to bridge the gap between the Inventory and the Ideal Inventory? What matters to you in life? If you were completely you, what would your life look like?

EXERCISE: Setting Values

This exercise is very simple: Articulate your values. Write them down, draw them, or type them up in a place you can easily access. Make sure you can edit them. They'll evolve. Here are some tips for setting values:

1. Your values don't have to be right or perfect. They're directions that help to guide you when you take steps in each moment of your life. As you take those steps, you may see that their consequences aren't moving you in the direction you want to go in life. So modify your values.

2. Values help you make tough decisions in the present that contribute to health and happiness over the long term. They're not there to make you feel good. Learning how to experience sadness, loss, pain, suffering, anger, and the entire range of emotions we experience is very useful for health and happiness. So don't pursue compulsions as values. If you want to value not feeling anxiety or not being wrong or anything that involves not feeling or thinking something, you're screwed.

3. Values translate into actions. Try to go beyond adjectives. A sunset is nice. You're nice. But what do you do? You might use a broad descriptor for a value, but make sure you know what specific actions that term translates into on a daily basis.

4. Values aren't an excuse to judge yourself and engage in more compulsions. If you recognize that you didn't act in line with your values, be mindful of that. It happened. You're probably experiencing the natural consequences of that step off your path, which is why you're aware of it. But it's in the past now. What matters is that the next step you take is toward the direction you want to move in life.

5. Values adapt easily to different situations. If you notice yourself getting overly specific, consider why you value that specific thing. Do you value getting promoted at work? Or is that simply a goal that's aligned with your value of taking care of your family, and you see the work promotion as a means by which you can take care of your family? If that's the case, then I'd suggest not getting too attached to the promotion. At this moment, that might be a way that you can take care of your family, but as the context around you changes, better ways to take care of your family may present themselves. You don't want to be blindly pursuing that promotion if the company is failing or they're asking you to do things that take you away from your family. If we pursue a tactic or a goal, we can miss the things we actually value.

MENTAL HEALTH IS THE PRACTICE OF BEING YOURSELF

STEP 6

Focus on changing actions, not thoughts or feelings

> When facing difficult situations, I realized that saying "I can't"
> usually means I don't want to do something because of the
> possibility of experiencing a particular feeling or result I might
> not like. So if I want to move forward and past challenges,
> then I have to decide if experiencing and learning how to deal
> with these feelings and uncertainties is something I'm willing
> to do.
>
> —KIANNI

If you want to improve your mental health, it helps if you're not investing heavily in making your mental health worse. Like we explored
in the chapter on mindfulness, if you practice distracting yourself for
several hours every day, it's only natural that you become very skilled
at being distracted. If you want to be a professional video game player
but you spend all of your time singing in karaoke bars, you're going
to be good at karaoke, not video games. Hopefully this is not a shocking
realization.

When we want to build better mental health and do more of the
things that matter to us in life, it's important that we stop taking steps

in the opposite direction. That's why cutting out compulsions is so important. Compulsions are the coping, checking, and controlling we engage in as a reaction to uncertainty, anxiety, and other feelings we don't like. The more we engage in the compulsions, the more we have those experiences we don't like. But understanding the connection between the compulsions and their effects isn't always obvious.

Imagine we're in a hot, sunny place. There's a big pool underneath some palm trees, lounge chairs all around it, beautiful hibiscus plants with bright pink flowers. The buzz of cicadas fades into the afternoon heat and the clink of ice in sweaty glasses dances through the air as you close your eyes and relax by the pool. At least, you try to relax, but it's difficult because there's this guy running around the pool jumping and shouting.

He yells out: "I LOVE JUMPING IN THE WATER!" And then he cannonballs into the pool. A big splash throws water on everybody around. Immediately, he's pulling himself out of the pool, shouting angrily, "I HATE GETTING WET! WHY DOES THIS ALWAYS HAPPEN TO ME?! ALL I WANTED TO DO WAS JUMP IN THE WATER! I DIDN'T ASK TO GET WET!"

He grabs a towel and furiously dries himself off, muttering about how terrible he feels. "If only there was something I could do to get rid of this nasty feeling. It doesn't feel right. I wish I felt like I did when I was getting ready to jump in the pool. I was so happy. Being wet just isn't me. I'm not my normal, dry self now. I wish there was something I could do so I didn't feel like this anymore. I should really do something I enjoy, something for me, like jumping in the pool. I love that feel of jumping in the pool. Things feel right when I'm jumping."

He runs a lap around the pool and belly flops off the diving board with a wet *smack*.

He charges back out of the pool again, growling, "EVERYTHING I LOVE ALWAYS GETS RUINED!"

This pattern will repeat itself until he's used up all of the towels, or he knocks himself unconscious diving into the shallow end, or somebody locks him in the pool house, or he simply wastes the rest of his life running in circles—jumping in the water, hating how he feels, trying to get rid of that feeling, jumping in again, and then hating how he feels again.

That was me when I struggled with my mental health.

Jumping in the water and getting wet are not separate. Liking compulsions but hating the outcomes is no less absurd than somebody who likes jumping in the water but hates getting wet. He needs to stop jumping in the pool.

While it's easy to spot the connection between jumping in the water and getting wet, it might not seem so obvious when it comes to dealing with the compulsions that are dumping you in the deep end of life. To make those connections, it's helpful to identify patterns of thinking and behaving that aren't helping you. It's how and why you do or use something that creates the problems.

SIMPLE PATTERNS OF THINKING AND BEHAVING

I don't talk much about specific mental illness diagnoses because I don't find them particularly useful or scientific. For example, if you're afraid of people disliking you, and meeting new people makes you anxious, so you try to control that anxiety by avoiding social situations, and you go to a doctor for help with that, the doctor might diagnose you with social anxiety disorder.

But if your reaction to that anxiety about being disliked is to compulsively clean yourself because you believe you could pass along a disease to others and kill them and then everybody would hate you, you'd probably get diagnosed with OCD.

However, if your reaction to that same anxiety is to get drunk in social situations and you always need to be drunk before getting into any intimate situation with another person because you're afraid of rejection, then you'd probably get diagnosed with the euphemistic-sounding alcohol use disorder.

Or if you try to control your anxiety about being disliked by engaging in restrictive eating compulsions because you think controlling your weight is a way to control what others think about you, then you'd probably get diagnosed with an eating disorder.

Mental illness diagnoses are based on superficially identifiable or self-reported symptoms. If we did that with physical illnesses, when you were suffering from pneumonia, you'd walk out of the doctor's office with a leaky nose disease, a coughing syndrome, a muscle ache disorder, and a body temperature dysregulation disability. Your doctor could give you medication to reduce the symptoms of all four of those, but that might not do anything about the monster chewing on you: the infection in your lungs.

In the examples of mental illness diagnoses I mentioned, it's the exact same behavior each time: experiencing uncertainty and feelings you don't like (in this case, related to being disliked by other people), then wanting to escape them—to find "peace of mind," chase certainty, etc.—and then engaging in compulsions to pursue those desires.

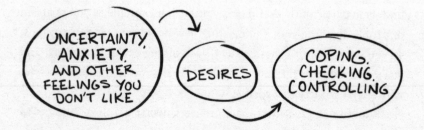

We also want to look at what brought on those feelings you don't like. So we'll take this system back a bit further, to the experiences we have and the judgments we make about those experiences that lead to the uncertainty, anxiety, and other feelings we don't like:

You start by having an experience. Let's say it's an internal experience, like a memory pops into your head about a time when another kid at school mocked you for making a mistake when you were reading in class. You judge that memory as meaning something about you. You judge yourself as somebody who always makes mistakes when you're stressed. You judge being judged as a very bad thing. That makes you anxious. It just so happens that today you're giving a presentation at work that you don't feel prepared to give. You're uncertain about whether you can do it well, and you worry that people will judge you negatively. You want people to think good things about you. You want to avoid mistakes and embarrassment. So you start on your usual compulsions to pursue those desires and eliminate those feelings you don't like.

The specific experiences, feelings, or compulsions DO NOT MATTER. You can fill in the blanks with any combination of experiences and compulsions. We'll come back to this, but when you're cutting out compulsions with the exercises coming up, map them out using this system to see opportunities for change. Recognize the experiences you're having. See the judgments you're making. Identify the uncertainties you're trying to eliminate. Understand the compulsions you engage in as a reaction to all of that.

To help with understanding the compulsive patterns of behavior and thinking, I approach them as three overlapping categories. I'll give an overview of them below and then we'll explore each one in depth in the steps ahead.

COPING, CHECKING, AND CONTROLLING

When I struggled with mental illness, it might have seemed like I had so many compulsions—checking door locks, Googling disease symptoms, not touching raw meat, checking for text messages, un-plugging appliances, binge eating, not holding knives when other people were around, rereading e-mails compulsively to look for errors, lying to control what others thought about me, avoiding people, needing to have everything "right" before I could start working or studying, compulsively washing my hands to get rid of germs, and the list went on. It could be daunting to deal with so many compulsions, but I actually didn't have so many. I had only three.

Coping, checking, and controlling are patterns of thinking and behaving. It doesn't matter what the compulsions look like superficially. They can happen entirely inside your head or entirely outside your head. They can affect only you or they can affect other people. They can be things you think of as "good" or "bad." Let's take a look at these three patterns:

1. **Coping** is all about trying to replace feelings or thoughts that you don't like. It's like trying to do yoga to calm yourself down when a hippo is attacking you. Many things we use to cope might seem "healthy," while others, like indulging in drugs or alcohol or junk food, are generally recognized as not so healthy. But the pattern is the problem. If my response to feeling bad is always to make myself feel good, what am I teaching my brain about how to make me feel good? That I need to feel bad first. Coping behaviors reward our brains for experiences we hate.

2. **Checking** is about trying to eliminate uncertainty. Many of us spend all day training our brains to check. It's very easy to check things in our connected world. You can pop open a dating app to

quickly check if somebody likes you. You can send a message to a friend after a drunken night out to check if she's angry with you. You can post pictures and videos to check if people think you're attractive. You can instantly check your bank account to make sure that dodgy store you went to didn't overcharge you. You can watch your home online. You can post questions on forums to get reassurance from thousands of people. You can check page after page of information about symptoms to make sure you don't have a deadly disease or you're not going insane. You can check the news. You can check unending streams of analytical data about who's doing what, where, whenever. With all of this checking, it's no wonder our brains keep giving us more uncertainties to check.

3. **Controlling** is all about trying to prevent experiences we don't like. Unfortunately, in the process of trying to control, we actually cause those experiences or even worse experiences to happen. Lying and manipulating what we tell others is a very common way this exhibits itself. Lying to make people like us typically leads to them not liking us. We often try to control others to relieve our own uncertainties. You can see this in any group when one member tries to control the others as a reaction to fear of failure, or when parents hover over their children to relieve uncertainties about the children getting hurt (and the parents getting blamed for being bad parents), or with romantic partners trying to control each other to relieve their anxieties about not being adequate. Controlling is also at work in compulsions that involve violence, in all forms, against ourselves or others.

Now that we've gone over the three types of compulsions, it's time to identify the ones in your life that you want to cut out. We'll use the next exercise to do that. It will help you to see the steps you'll take in the weeks ahead to go where you want to be.

EXERCISE: The Hierarchy

This is a classic exposure and response prevention (ERP) exercise. A Hierarchy is a ranked list of compulsions. It's an effective tool because it helps to overcome a common challenge people run into when cutting out compulsions: they start with compulsions they don't yet have the skills or emotional fitness capacity to cut out.

For instance, a woman who's struggling with commitment might go to a therapist and ask for help with learning how to stop ditching her romantic partners. To her, that seems like the behavior she wants to cut out. She wants to learn how to sit with uncertainty about her partner being "the one." But as she digs into her reactions to other uncertainties in her life, she might discover that she's always jumping from job to job, she often changes plans or cancels on friends at the last minute, she won't go to a restaurant without researching the menu in advance to make her selection, she once spent an hour at the pharmacy trying to decide between two different brands of identical cough medicine.

Although a recent relationship experience might be creating significant amounts of anxiety or regret, reacting to uncertainty about choices and commitments is common throughout her life, not only in relationships. If she wants to handle that uncertainty about long-term relationships, she'll benefit from first learning how to cut out compulsions around relatively small choices, like picking something off a menu or finishing a project at work.

The Hierarchy helps us lay out all of our compulsions so we can see the path from where we are to where we want to be. You can do this exercise on paper or with sticky notes or you can do it using a spreadsheet to make it easy to move the items around as you rank them. Here's how you do the Hierarchy:

1. Make a list of all the compulsions you engage in to cope with, check on, or control uncertainty, anxiety, and other feelings you don't like.
   - Refer back to the Inventory exercise if you need a reminder of how you're spending your time.
   - Be specific. Something like "compulsions at work" is too vague. Articulate each of the compulsions at work, e.g., "avoiding my boss," "using 'Reply All' unnecessarily," "procrastinating by using social media," "lying to customers," etc.

2. Rank the compulsions based on how difficult you think it would be to cut them out. You could give the most difficult a 10, the easiest a 1, and rank the others accordingly.
   - You'll have many compulsions of equivalent difficulty.
   - If you're stuck on where to start ranking, pick two at random and ask yourself which would be more difficult to eliminate. Imagine the practical changes involved and how much anxiety you would experience if you couldn't do that action ever again. Continue with that ranking process until you've sorted through the heap of compulsions.

3. Start working through the compulsions, cutting out one each week, starting from the easiest and working your way up.

4. It's also useful to look at your Ideal Inventory and create a Reverse Hierarchy—a ranked list of all the things you want to do more of in your life. As you cut out one compulsion each week, you can also add in one activity you want to do more of.

As we progress through the following chapters on coping, checking, and controlling, you'll learn specific skills to support yourself through the process of cutting out those compulsions and doing more of what matters to you.

Here's an example of what a Hierarchy can look like:

DIFFICULTY	COMPULSION
10	Checking the stove
8	Not driving
8	Avoiding touching "contaminated" things
7	Leaving my home messy so I have an excuse not to invite people over
7	Not cooking for others / not giving them food
7	Checking myself in every reflective surface I pass
7	Washing until I feel clean
6	Lying about what I like or dislike
6	Ending every relationship the moment I think something is wrong
6	Only eating frozen food / not touching raw meat
5	Not asking people for things I want
5	Not leaving social events when I want to because I'm afraid of what people will think or say about me
5	Boredom binge eating
4	Saving every receipt
4	Staying up for hours online instead of going to bed
4	Checking my lock at the gym / stopping my workout early to check my locker
3	Avoiding responsibility at work so I can criticize whomever does take responsibility
3	Avoiding bills / finances
3	Not writing e-mails until I feel "ready" to write them
2	Procrastinating on chores
2	Rewriting and rereading e-mails
1	Stalking social media profiles of people I like
1	Checking door and window locks

*

With that Hierarchy example, I would start with the lock-checking compulsions at the bottom and then work my way up, cutting out one compulsion or a set of related compulsions each week. Keep in mind that this example is probably a bit on the short side. You'll likely have more compulsions, but don't get hung up on trying to figure them all out before you get started. You'll discover things to add to your Hierarchy as you move through it. You'll adjust your rankings as you run into challenges.

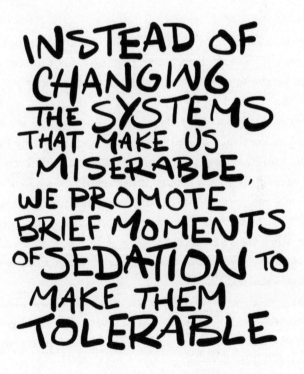

INSTEAD OF CHANGING THE SYSTEMS THAT MAKE US MISERABLE, WE PROMOTE BRIEF MOMENTS OF SEDATION TO MAKE THEM TOLERABLE

STEP 7

Stop coping

It's easy to teach a puppy to pee on your sofa: give it a cookie every time it pees on the sofa. Even better, take it out for a run only after it has peed on the sofa. You don't like it when your puppy pees on the sofa? Is that stressful for you? Then don't do things that it likes only after it does things you don't like.

Cookies are delicious and puppies are poor at setting limits for delicious things, so that puppy will pee on your sofa even when it doesn't necessarily need a cookie. It likes getting them long after it's full. So it'll keep peeing on the sofa more and more. It might even pretend to pee on the sofa when there's no pee to pee. Puppies can seem so clever when they want a cookie.

Imagine if you rewarded your brain with things it likes only after it did things you dislike.

That's exactly what we're doing with coping behaviors. They might make you feel good, but they also send a very clear message to your brain: if you feel something I don't like, I'll give you something you like to get rid of those feelings.

Coping makes unhappiness and illness the prerequisites for happiness and health.

WHAT I'M TALKING ABOUT WHEN
I'M TALKING ABOUT COPING

Eliminating coping doesn't necessarily mean cutting out the things we're using or doing to cope. It's important not to conflate the things with the behavioral pattern. Again: it's not the *what* that matters, it's the *how* and the *why*.

When I refer to coping, I'm referring to a pattern of experiencing thoughts or feelings we don't like and then doing something to replace those unwanted experiences with other experiences we think we want. Coping might involve traveling halfway around the world to ride an elephant, or staying at home to watch TV shows all night, or doing yoga, doing heroin, cutting yourself, playing video games, gardening, going shopping, eating an entire pizza and a box of cookies—whatever it is that you do to cover up loneliness, sedate your fears, quiet the voice in your head, or mask your insecurities.

Yes, I put drugs, yoga, self-harm, and elephant riding in the same category *if* they're attempts to escape feelings because then they're not different actions. They're the same action: trying to escape feelings.

I'm not suggesting that pattern isn't considered "normal." It's arguably the basis for most marketing: Feel something bad and buy this thing to feel good again! Beer ads tell you to unwind at the end of a stressful week. Supplements promise to eliminate your stress "naturally." Resorts encourage you to "get away from it all." Food companies bait you with sweet indulgences as a reward for enduring pain. The message: get attacked by a monster, buy a new dress to replace the blood-and-guts-stained one, and then everything will be okay.

When you've felt down or sad or stressed or anxious, it's likely you've rewarded your brain. You've tried to unwind, stay "balanced," relax, mix things up. When your brain feels something you don't like, do you give it a cookie (figuratively or literally)? You're laying out a clear path to rewards, and that path goes straight through stress, poor communication, damaged relationships, hatred, jealousy, self-loathing, and peeing on furniture.

Instead of changing the systems that make us miserable, we promote brief moments of sedation to make them tolerable.

We need to change those systems.

BUT AREN'T SOME COPING BEHAVIORS BETTER THAN OTHERS?

As long as we practice compulsive patterns as a reaction to feelings we don't like, we're always in danger of relapse. It's as if you were compulsively hitting yourself in the face with a hammer so we swapped out the metal hammer for a soft, inflatable toy hammer. You do, however, continue to swing something at your face. Only now you don't experience the same nasty consequences. That can be an important step to take, so if that's where you're at, that is awesome. It's extremely difficult to take that first step away from old destructive habits. But keep going. You need to eliminate the pattern of behavior. You need to stop swinging at your face.

As long as you swing the compulsion hammer at yourself, even if it's with a "healthier" hammer, you're stuck in the same old pattern. And when life happens, as it inevitably does, and somebody comes up to you and swaps your soft hammer for a sledgehammer, you're right back to where you were, possibly even worse, looking for a way to deal with your smashed-up head.

Let stress and anxiety and suffering point you to the problem. They are not the problem. They are symptoms. They're big arrows pointing to whatever it is that needs to change. Sometimes those changes are major shifts in the systems we interact with in society, at school, in relationships, or wherever we may be. Racism, sexism, homophobia, poverty, mental illness stigma—these are all big, systemic problems. They're like crowds of people rushing up to you and smashing you over the head with sledgehammers. We are not responsible for the pain they cause us, but merely coping with that pain cultivates those problems. We need to work with others to change those systems.

At other times, like when you engage in compulsions, you're creating the pain. That's when you're hitting yourself in the head with the hammer. You don't need painkillers or extra bandages or special mantras to help erase the pain so you can keep smashing yourself in the face. You don't have a bloody face personality disorder. You need to stop swinging hammers at your own feelings.

SO SHOULD I STOP DOING YOGA AND EATING HEALTHY?

No, that's not what I'm saying. Do them because they're beneficial to your health, not as a reaction to something you don't like. **The activity is not the problem.**

If somebody feels stressed at work and then does drugs to escape that feeling, he's engaging in the same behavioral pattern as somebody who feels stressed at work and then does yoga to escape that feeling. Neither is addressing the source of the stress at work. It will only grow. Whatever they're doing for relief will eventually stop delivering relief at the same level it did in the past. That is doubly problematic with healthy activities like exercise because you might stop exercising if it stops "working" or if you no longer feel stressed. Exercise is beneficial to decreasing your risk of disease and early death, regardless of what's happening in your life. On the flip side, being sedentary increases your risk of disease and early death, regardless of whether you like sitting.

SO WHAT ARE YOU SUPPOSED TO DO WHEN YOU GET ANXIOUS OR DEPRESSED OR STRESSED?

Feel them. You're human. You have feelings. You have thoughts. You have urges. Once you're experiencing them, they're there. You can experience them, fully, without trying to do anything to them or because of them.

Have you ever been to a Japanese *onsen*? They're baths fed by geothermally heated water gurgling up from deep in the earth. I lived in Japan for a couple of years and I miss the hot spring baths so much. But I didn't like them at first. They were too hot! Much hotter than any water I had ever touched that wasn't boiling on the stove top. I wanted to be clean, not poached.

When we dip a foot into anxiety, or guilt, or loneliness, or anger, or any other pool of feelings we've learned to avoid, it's much like somebody touching a hot spring bath for the first time. Alarms go off in our brains—we'll be hurt and damaged if we step deeper into this feeling. Pull your foot out!

Of course, millions of people all over the world love soaking in hot spring baths. Once I learned to not pull my foot back but to instead get in the water—all the way in—it actually became a very pleasurable experience. Now it's something I look forward to and choose to do. One big difference between hot spring water and the experiences you don't like is that getting into a hot spring bath is a choice. You don't actually have a choice about the experiences you don't like unless you want to get stuck in life. Everything you want to do in life is on the other side of an enormous bath full of thoughts and feelings you've tried to avoid.

This is where the work comes in to build your emotional fitness level. Get naked. Get in. And get soaking. You'll notice this experience will be very physical. You'll experience these feeling or thoughts in the same way you'd feel hot water. It'll be all over your body and your immediate reaction will be to get away from them. Let yourself soak in them. You can be you in them. You can enjoy stepping into them and out of them as you move on to doing what you value in life.

ACCEPTANCE AND COMMITMENT THERAPY (ACT)

Developed by professor, researcher, clinical psychologist, author, and creator of great metaphors Dr. Steven C. Hayes, ACT is a form of therapy that increases psychological flexibility by focusing on six core processes: acceptance, cognitive defusion, being present, self as context, values, and committed action. This is all to help people move toward difficult experiences instead of narrowing their world through avoidance. ACT recognizes that we create mental health challenges for ourselves by conflating our identity with our thoughts, by rigidly judging our experiences, by trying to avoid those experiences, and by wrapping our lives up in restrictive, unhelpful narratives we tell ourselves about ourselves. The way out of that trap is to ACT:

> Accept your reactions and be present.
> Choose a valued direction.
> Take action.

To fit the language I'm using in this book and for the purposes of the examples coming up, I'm modifying the wording of the ACT algorithm to:

> I accept the stuff in my head and bring my awareness to the present.
> I choose a direction aligned with my values.
> I take action.

You'll see this format when we go through the examples of cutting out compulsions.

I discovered Dr. Hayes's work when I began participating in mental health patient communities online. ACT resonated with me because I'd seen in my own life the effectiveness of these techniques. It also struck me as the personal, therapeutic approach to dealing with the same challenges I was learning to help companies overcome in my work with Tom Wujec. Innovation, whether it's personal or professional, is all about stepping into a hot bath of experiences you don't like and letting your values guide your actions when you want to fall back on what you've done before, even though what you've done before has nearly destroyed you or, in the business context, your company.

Much of what I'm doing throughout this book is melding design thinking and change management tools with an ACT approach to handling the stuff in our heads. I can't give you a complete view of ACT or design thinking in this book so I encourage you to continue exploring these practices. They are deep and useful.

THE PRACTICE OF ELIMINATING A COPING COMPULSION

You might not be ready to jump into the hottest water, which is why we did the Hierarchy exercise to figure out the easier compulsions to tackle first. Begin with something small and work up your capacity to deal with the tougher compulsions. Make it as easy as possible for yourself by starting with something "normal." It might be that you always play video games or watch videos before you feel "ready" to do your work. Maybe you automatically start flipping through social media channels because you don't want to feel bored (even though what you really need to do is your laundry because you're down to your last pair of underwear and you're rewearing socks you wore last week).

One of the "normal" coping behaviors I always got caught up in was watching videos online. I'd be stressed or bored and I'd tell myself that if I just watched another couple of music videos or another episode of a Japanese cartoon or maybe a few funny comedy videos, then I'd feel better, I would have unwound from the stressful, boring day, I would feel motivated, and then I could accomplish whatever it was I needed to accomplish, even things I didn't want to do. Of course, it never worked out that way. I'd spend the rest of the night watching videos and being angry at myself for not getting anything done that I actually wanted to do.

Using the ACT structure, I'll show you how I approach cutting out coping compulsions like distracting myself online. Here's how I do it:

I accept the stuff in my head and bring my awareness to the present

- I get home after a busy day at work. I need to buy groceries so I can make food for myself for the week, but I don't feel like going to the store. I want to watch videos. I don't want to do more work.

- The stuff in my head doesn't need to change. My brain can think of reasons to put off going to the grocery store: I'll wake up earlier tomorrow morning and jog to the store! I've been meaning to start jogging so this is the perfect opportunity! My brain loves to rationalize me into problems. That's okay. Those thoughts can be there. I feel tired and stressed and that's fine, too. Those feelings can be there.

- Watching the videos is the coping compulsion. There's nothing wrong with watching videos.* The problem here is wanting to watch videos

---

* Please watch my online videos (after you get the groceries).

to change how I feel before I do something I need to do. I know it's easy to get sucked into the black hole of the Internet if I do that. There'll always be one more video I can watch before I feel ready. It could be hours until I feel like going to the store, if I ever do go.

I choose a direction aligned with my values

- Do I value watching kitten videos or taking care of my health and my finances? Not only will the groceries help me prepare healthy lunches to eat at work, but I'll also save money. If I spend the night watching kitten videos, there's no way that will actually contribute anything to my life that I care about. I might feel good in the short term, sure. Maybe somebody will give me a trophy for that. But I'll be upset the next day and stressed out and I'll be eating some junk food in the windowless basement food court of an office building and then I'll pass out in the afternoon at my desk in a carb coma, which will make me even more stressed because I'll end up only more behind at work.

I take action

- I don't watch the videos. Even though it's difficult, I'll choose the action (getting groceries) that will help me move toward my values (being healthy, making smart financial decisions, etc.). I walk out the door carrying my reusable grocery bag, dragging my screaming brain.

- When I eliminate coping compulsions and align my actions with my values, I'll feel withdrawal. My brain will thrash around and demand to get fed compulsions. It'll throw thoughts and feelings at me that I don't like. But I don't have to chase after anything my brain throws up. I can practice mindfulness, being present as I get groceries, as I interact with my community, and when I return and prepare food for myself. I can enjoy all of that experience as I act according to my values.

You can apply this practice anywhere as you build up your skills. You can see the basics there of building your emotional fitness capacity. Your brain will try to get you to avoid difficult experiences by getting you to do something that feels good but you don't care about. And you can thank your brain for that, and take those feelings with you while you head off to do what you value.

You've already got a list of compulsions there in your Hierarchy that you can cut out using this ACT approach. Many of the feelings you experience as you work through that list will be intense. You could be doing something like going online constantly to check dating apps and social media sites for messages to reassure yourself that you won't be alone. When you cut out a compulsion like that, you'll come up against that fear of being alone and it can be terrifying. In the chapters coming up we'll look more at how to lift those heavy fears and carry them with us in life. We'll also look at handling other difficult experiences like sounds, physical sensations, tastes, or visual stimuli that you've developed compulsions around. But right now, to help with any compulsion you're tackling, I'll explain an exercise that's especially helpful if you continually find yourself relapsing into a compulsion you want to cut out.

EXERCISE: Take a Compulsion Journey

This is a design-thinking exercise I first learned from Tom Wujec as a tool to help companies innovate in a way that fits with their customers' lives. When you're doing it with customers, it's often referred to as a Customer Journey or a Journey Map, and it's how you map out a current or potential customer's day to understand all sorts of things: why she's not buying from you, how you can help her with challenges she has before or after buying from you, how you can innovate to meet other needs she has, etc.

We'll adapt this exercise to do something very innovative as well: help you cut out compulsions. We'll do that by mapping out everything that happens leading up to a compulsion. By visualizing the complete system around it, we can see opportunities to make changes that might be easier than trying to stop yourself when you're on the verge of a compulsion or deep into it and those addictive loops are already spinning in your head. Here's how it works:

1. Grab something to draw and write with and a piece of paper large enough for you to draw a complete day. The bigger the paper, the better.

2. Somewhere on the far right side, draw or write the compulsion you're cutting out. It could be any compulsion: drinking booze, watching TV, masturbating to porn, praying, scrolling through social media, doing drugs, binge eating, harming yourself, trolling, knitting, etc.

3. From the compulsion, draw a squiggly line around the page. I like to put the compulsion in the bottom right corner and then I draw my squiggly line across the page to the top left corner. Like this:

4. Now, along the squiggly line, draw and write what hap-
    pened during the day before the compulsion started. Here
    are some events and experiences you might want to illus-
    trate:

    a. What did you do right before you started engaging in
        the compulsion? What were you doing an hour before
        that?

    b. Why were you in the place where you engaged in the
        compulsion?

    c. How did your emotions change throughout the day?
        What did you feel and when did you feel it?

    d. When did you eat? What did you eat?

    e. What time did you wake up? How did you feel when
        you woke up?

    f. What unexpected events happened during the day?

    g. How did other people affect you?

    h. What challenges did you encounter? Did you overcome
        them? Did they throw you off course?

    i. What worked well? What did you enjoy?

    j. What facilitated or enabled the compulsion? Were there
        other people involved? Did you need equipment to help
        you do it? If so, what made that equipment accessible?

k. What external social or economic pressures are affecting you?

l. What happened yesterday that affected today?

5. Once the day is completely mapped out, look for where the compulsions actually started. For instance, if you had to pick up alcohol to drink, the compulsion might have started when you convinced yourself you needed to stop by the drugstore, which just happens to be beside the store where you always buy wine. Or maybe the compulsion started when you came home and automatically turned on your computer like you always do as soon as you walk through the door.

6. That point you identify shows you where you can make changes earlier in the system of your day to prevent yourself getting pushed into a situation where it's more difficult to stop the compulsion. That point may also show you how to predict and prevent relapses. For example, you might see that every time you get drunk, you relapse afterward, either immediately or the next morning when you're hungover. That doesn't necessarily mean you need to stop drinking, but it shows you where you can proactively bring in supports to help you prevent relapse. That might be as simple as making sure you schedule time with friends the morning after you drink so that you're not stuck home alone with your brain wanting to do whatever compulsions you fall back into.

Break the IF X THEN Y thinking pattern

> Getting better meant that I had to step back from the horror
> movies that ran on autopilot in my head all day long. I couldn't
> stop the thoughts and the more I tried the worse they got. This
> is where mindfulness made the difference. Once I became
> mindfully aware of the thoughts, I placed myself in a position
> of power—I gave myself a choice as to where I wanted to focus
> my attention: focus on trying to alleviate the fear or focus on
> what I needed to do to conquer this hell in my head. Every day
> I do my best to place myself in that position of power.
>
> —SOPHIE

There's a simple pattern at work when we're coping, checking, and controlling: IF X THEN Y. You could see it back there in the chapter on coping compulsions: IF X (I feel bad) THEN Y (I need to do something to change that feeling). This pattern triggers anger and violence, it's the flimsy foundation that keeps collapsing underneath your sinking self-esteem, and it's the equation that leaves you ruminating for hours and hours. It leads to dependencies, it feeds depression, it's what drives every compulsion you can imagine, physical or mental. It's a very simple, toxic pattern that can consume our lives. It's like running your life on an ancient computer program that produces nothing but errors. In fact, if you've ever learned any computer programming, it's likely that one of the basic techniques you learned early on was the IF-THEN statement. It's a conditional expression in the code that essentially tells the computer IF a thing matches some criteria, THEN do or don't do some other thing. IF X THEN Y.

This tiny little program in my brain almost crashed my life. It ruled my behaviors. Take a look at the list below and see if you can spot familiar ideas:

IF X THEN Y IN ACTION

- IF I leave the stove on, THEN my building will burn down.

- IF I burn down my building, THEN everybody will hate me.

- IF I check the door lock, THEN my kids are safe.

- IF that guy makes eye contact with me, THEN I must be attractive.

- IF I look attractive, THEN I won't die alone.

- IF I get criticized at work, THEN I'll get fired (and go broke and end up on the street homeless and I'll get HIV and I'll be murdered and nobody will like me).

- IF I wash my hands under scalding hot water, THEN they won't have germs on them.

- IF I do mindfulness right, THEN I won't be stressed anymore.

- IF she doesn't respond to my text message immediately, THEN she's having an affair (or she's died in a car accident, or both).

- IF I can't remember what happened, THEN I must have done something terrible.

- IF I don't check to see if my teeth are clean, THEN there'll be something stuck in them and people will think I'm gross and they'll talk about me behind my back.

- IF I say no to people, THEN they won't like me and they'll think I'm lazy (and I'll get fired).

- IF I mention this problem to my colleague, THEN it won't be my responsibility later when it blows up.

- IF I stop the kids from doing anything risky, THEN they won't get hurt and I won't get blamed for it.

- IF I check the mail, THEN I might get a bill for something unexpected and I'll go broke.

- IF people don't act a certain way toward me, THEN they're disrespecting me.

- IF I get the right car or the right shoes or the right phone or the right home or the right shiny whatever, THEN people will like me and be impressed by me.

- IF I have thoughts of harming somebody, THEN I'm a horrible person.

- IF I don't get rid of these thoughts, THEN I'll never be able to live the life I want.

- IF I do compulsions for an hour, THEN I can do my work without distraction.

- IF everything else around me changed, THEN my life would be better.

- IF I could find the right medication, THEN I wouldn't have these mental health challenges.

IS YOUR WORLD BUILT ON MAGICAL THINKING?

In psychology, the term "magical thinking" typically refers to something like a girl believing she can prevent her parents from getting into a car accident if she prays in a particular way without having any impure thoughts. IF X (I pray correctly and purely) THEN Y (my parents will be safe). This also logically implies that IF X (I pray incorrectly and blasphemously) THEN Y (I'll be responsible for my parents' death). If she enjoys the sense of relief and certainty she gets when she does the prayer "correctly," she's setting herself up for the inevitable but totally logical anxiety that will result when she does it "incorrectly." She's guaranteed to have thoughts she judges as impure, which will lead to repeating the prayers over and over again to get them "right."

This is the trap of magical thinking. If you believe the action will prevent what you're afraid of, you're setting up your brain to believe that not performing that action will cause your fears to come true. And then when you don't perform that action, or don't perform it correctly, you panic and anxiety spikes; it's as though not performing that action were equivalent to making your fears coming true. And this extends way beyond things people consider "magical" or "delusional."

It's the same pattern at work if you believe you need to change your body to look a particular way before people will love you or value you. This is a belief that supplement companies, gyms, the media, your friends, and your family members may all participate in promoting. But it's delusional. It's a belief that rituals will control the thoughts of others. And it's a trap. If you tell your brain you must look a particular way to be valued, then you logically set yourself up not to feel valued if you don't look that way.

If you believe your partner loves you because he sends you lengthy messages sprinkled with emojis, then it's only natural that you become anxious when he sends you short messages without emojis. If you want that warm, loving feeling you get when you open the loquacious, emoji-filled message, you're also choosing the panicked uncertainty of reading a one-word reply or, heaven forbid, no reply at all ☹.

It's this same pattern at work if you believe you need to drink alcohol or do drugs to be creative. Even if you simply believe you need the right kind of notebook, the right types of pens, or a perfectly quiet environment before you do any work, you're walking right into the trap. You'll have to drink more and more, or get higher and higher, or find a quieter and quieter place, until you stop creating completely because your brain won't let you satisfy the first part of the equation.

Like we discussed in the previous chapter, if you believe you need to have a specific feeling before you can do what matters to you, trying to chase that feeling consumes you and leaves nothing for what matters. When you cut out compulsions, you break that IF X THEN Y pattern.

SO WHAT'S THE ALTERNATIVE?

Luckily, the alternative is an equation with only one variable: IF X THEN X. That's it. Just X. No judgments, magical thinking, discrimination, or overreaction necessary. The antidote to the IF X THEN Y pattern of thinking is the practice of mindfulness. As you practice mindfulness and meditation more in your life, you're going to find that it becomes easier to break this pattern and simply be with the experience you're having.

In the past, you might have believed something like IF X (I feel stressed) THEN Y (I can't be myself around my friends), but now, if you feel stressed, that's great, you feel stressed. It doesn't have any meaning you don't give to it. You can do the things you care about while feeling stressed. This is mindfulness at work. You can have emotions or thoughts. What you choose to do while having those emotions or thoughts is entirely separate.

WHAT ABOUT SELF-ESTEEM?

I'm opposed to self-esteem. Or, I should say, I'm opposed to how we generally approach self-esteem, as a self-image propped up by this IF X THEN Y pattern. IF I get compliments, IF I make lots of money, IF I'm desired, IF I gain more followers, IF I get gold stars, IF people say I'm smart, IF I have the best titles, IF I get all the likes, IF I do it right, IF I'm invited to special events, IF I reach the goal, IF I'm better than you, IF I'm not wrong, IF I win . . . THEN I'm valuable.

The pursuit of self-esteem logically sets you up for low self-esteem. It's the same trap again: If you believe your value comes from people giving you things, then you hand over control of your self-image to other people. If they don't give you those things, then your brain logically concludes you must not be valuable. In this situation you can begin to see how chasing desirable feelings we think of as "good" can actually set us up for the feelings we don't like. You will spend much more time not getting compliments than you will spend getting compliments. So if your self-worth depends on compliments, expect your self-worth to be low.

Your value doesn't come from other people. If you hand over control of your value to others, expect them to waste it. They won't know you've put them in charge of the only thing you own. Take back your self. Remove self-esteem from the equation. You don't need to break yourself apart to find specks of gold. Your value is innate in your existence and it can only grow.

You are awesome. Proceed accordingly. The next exercise, the Awesome Schedule, will help you with that. We're doing this exercise here because it's such an effective way to bring healthy activities into your life without relying on that IF X THEN Y pattern. It's all about proactively doing the things you want to do as part of your life, instead of doing them reactively or waiting to do them until after you've captured some feeling.

EXERCISE: The Awesome Schedule

The Awesome Schedule is all about doing things that help you be healthy and happy regardless of how you feel or what's happening in your life. You can always support yourself. It's not something you do after you get a special feeling or reach a particular point in life. You can start doing it right now.

The Awesome Schedule is a simple way of helping you support the practice of being yourself (which is awesome). Here's how:

1. Grab a calendar or open up your digital schedule. Make sure you're doing this exercise in something you already use. If you don't use a calendar to schedule in events, grab some sticky notes you can post in a visible location. Also grab some paper you can brainstorm on, or use the sticky notes.

2. Consider your values. Take a look at your Ideal Inventory exercise. Consider the experiences you've had in life with which you felt especially engaged or happy.

3. What types of activities support any or all of those? What activities help you be healthy and happy? What do you always enjoy doing? What do you wish you did more often? You might want to write them down on a piece of paper so you can brainstorm a bit here. Write down whatever comes to mind. Just get it out of your head and onto paper.

4. Of the activities that you wrote down, pick one that you enjoy doing simply for its own sake. Make sure it's something you can do.

5. Commit to doing that once per month. Schedule it in. How will you make that a regular part of your life?

6. Do it.

7. Keep adding to your Awesome Schedule as you show yourself that you can do things you enjoy, not to control your feelings or to get things, but as an expression of who you are.

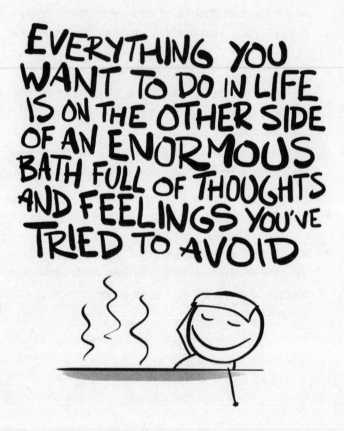

STEP 9

Stop checking

That very first exercise we did at the beginning of the book—to not check your phone when you get the urge to check it—was an exercise to practice the basics of cutting out checking compulsions. You get an urge, you accept that it's there, and you choose how you want to act. It's an opportunity to break that IF X THEN Y pattern. You can experience an urge to check without reacting to it or trying to make it go away. Checking your phone might be something you consider "normal," but it's in those normal behaviors that we train our brains to react to uncertainty, anxiety, and other feelings we don't like. And I'm telling that to you as somebody who was on the extreme end of disordered checking.

Compulsively checking was a major part of my struggle with mental illness. I could spend hours online reloading sites and checking accounts for responses to messages or comments. I would set my alarm and then check that I'd set it, and then reset it and check again, and then set two or three more alarms because I wasn't certain I could be certain they were set. I checked every appliance and lock and plug in my home. I was constantly checking to see if I still had everything on me that I needed. I was checking how people were looking at me. I was checking memories of conversations over and over again to be certain I hadn't said something offensive or done something horrible. I was checking for reassurance, checking receipts, checking for stains, checking that my fly was up, checking how I smelled, and checking and checking. . . . But that was a practice I trained my brain into, built on a solid foundation of totally normal, socially acceptable checking.

WHERE IS MY WATER BOTTLE?

One night, I was walking home from the gym and I started to wonder if I'd put my water bottle back in my gym bag when I left the locker room. I'd recently forgotten my water bottle there and bought a new one—the nice shiny yellow one I was now worried I'd forgotten.

So there was an uncertainty. It was something that had happened before. It had cost me money—not much, but money I didn't need to spend. I would feel even worse if I had to spend more money on another water bottle simply because I hadn't paid attention. This isn't delusional. Worrying that I forgot my water bottle is a "legitimate worry," right?

To add some context to this situation: I'd been recovered from mental illness for about six years, around the time I was writing this book. At that time, under no criteria would I have classified myself as having any mental illness. I'd say I was physically and mentally in great shape. I was a totally sane, rational human being worried about forgetting something. All I had to do was open my gym bag and check if the bottle was there. I was still close enough to the gym that I could run back and grab it.

Let's pause here. What would you do in this situation? Based on everything you've read so far, what do you think I did?

I didn't check. I kept on walking. When I got home, I put my bag down and still didn't open it. Later, when I wanted a drink, I pulled my water bottle out of my bag.

Checking my water bottle might not seem like it has anything to do with mental health. But if we look at the pattern of behavior there, what was happening? I experienced an uncertainty (what if I forgot my water bottle?) that triggered emotions I didn't like (fear of wasting money, fearing of losing something, fear of being responsible for something going wrong), and then I wanted to do something to get rid of those feelings.

Although it may seem "normal," checking for a water bottle would be no different from checking with three different doctors to make sure they all agree that your lymph nodes aren't abnormally swollen, or checking and rechecking the e-mail you just sent your boss to make sure you didn't make any mistakes that might get you fired, or checking the door and window locks multiple times before bed, or constantly seeking reassurance from your partner so you can be certain she still loves you.

I didn't check because I didn't want to train my brain to give me more uncertainties and more anxieties to chase after. If I had checked and it was there, I would've been happy. My brain would have registered that, and in the future, it would have given me more uncertainties so I could try to get rid of those and find the same happiness. If I had checked and the bottle wasn't there, I would have been upset and run back to the gym, and my brain would have registered that losing a water bottle is a very bad thing and we should worry about losing things even more in the future so we can avoid being responsible for bad things happening.

Brains are logical and helpful. When it comes to compulsions, even the compulsions that seem the most absurdly irrational grow very logically from reasonable, everyday activities. Let's look at an example of a helpful, logical brain doing what it does best:

THE TOTALLY LOGICAL PROGRESSION
OF A MENTAL ILLNESS

Assume I did check my bag. The bottle would be there and I'd feel relieved. But then my brain, helpful brain that it is, would want me to experience that amazing feeling of relief again. It might even try to help me get that experience right away by tossing out an uncertainty about my wallet and my keys. I always keep them in my gym bag, and as my hand was already in there, I should make sure they didn't get stolen at the gym. Losing my wallet or having somebody steal my keys to break into my apartment and take all of my valuables would be far worse than losing a water bottle, right? It only makes sense to check for those if I'm worried about losing a bottle.

And if losing valuables is a bad thing, well, there are so many different ways that could happen, so my brain would be on the lookout for other uncertainties that could lead to me losing resources. What if I left the patio door open? What if I didn't lock my gym locker? What if somebody copied my bank card? What if I didn't lock the front door when I left this morning? What if I left the car unlocked? What if the windows are all open? It'd be stupid if I was constantly checking my wallet but didn't check all of that other stuff. Somebody could walk right into my home or log in to my bank account and take everything I owned. That would be far more devastating than losing my wallet. So doesn't it make sense to check them every day?

At least, even if all of that did happen, I'd still have my job. I could make money to get my life back. But what if I lost my job? There are so many ways that could happen. What if I say something stupid in a meeting or an e-mail and everybody thinks I'm not a "good fit"? What if I say the wrong thing to a customer? What if something gets stolen and I get blamed for it? What if they find out I lied a bit (a lot) on my application? What if I miss an important deadline? What if somebody else on my team screws up and people think it's my fault? What if I damage something at work and I have to pay for it? What if I don't set the security alarm properly when I'm leaving? What if my laptop battery catches on fire and burns down the entire office? I left it plugged in and charging when I went to a meeting uptown, the meeting went late, so I wasn't going to return to the office and get it, but the adapter gets so hot when the laptop is charging, and laptop batteries do catch on fire. So should I go back to the office and get it? I planned to meet friends for dinner but I could tell them I'm working late. They'll understand.

At least the office building is empty at night and the company would have insurance, but what if I was responsible for burning down my apartment building? I'd be paying for that for the rest of my life. What if I left the toaster plugged in? What if I left my desktop computer running and it overheated? What if there was paper or cloth near something that could get hot? What if I spilled something flammable on the floor and a spark from a plug set off a fire? What if I left the stove on? If I'm going to check to make sure I didn't lose my water bottle, surely it's reasonable to check something as potentially damaging as the stove. There was this old stove in the apartment I was renting and it had knobs that could actually pop off—it had happened to me when I'd turned them too quickly. Then I couldn't know if it was actually turned to high or low or off or burn-the-building-the-fuck-down. So it made sense to check that the knobs were actually in the off position by wiggling them, then to wait for a bit and touch the burner to make sure it wasn't heating up. Because what if I'd actually turned it on by wiggling the knob to make sure it was off? At least one thing working in my favor was the fact that it was an electric stove, so when it was set to high, the burner would glow red-hot. To really make sure it wasn't on, all I had to do was wait in front of the stove and watch the burners to make sure they didn't turn red. But what if there was some type of malfunction inside? It's plugged into that big outlet in the back. If they couldn't even design the knobs well, is it inconceivable to think that the rest of the stove might be poorly designed?

What's stopping something from breaking inside of the stove, something I can't see or check, and turning the entire appliance into an apartment fire starter and burning up all of the old ladies and their cats? And it would be ALL MY FAULT.

Shouldn't everybody be standing in front of their stove right now watching it?

That's why I didn't check if my water bottle was in my bag.

TOWARD PLEASURE, AWAY FROM PAIN, INTO A BOTTOMLESS PIT

Every time you check, you validate a pattern that your brain will run with, very logically, finding more and more uncertainties, at ever-increasing levels of severity and complexity. It'll do it about losing valuables, relationships, freedom, reputation, health—whatever you decide is something you don't want to lose. Your brain will very logically and helpfully try to find all of the ways imaginable that you could lose those valuables. When you seek relief from uncertainty, you reinforce two feedback loops in your brain that guarantee more uncertainty.

The first loop is all about positive rewards. Relief from uncertainty will make me feel good! Now my brain needs to find more uncertainties so I can get that feeling I want by getting rid of them. Remember: Relief from uncertainty requires uncertainty. You're making uncertainty a prerequisite for feeling good.

It helped me to approach all of my mental health challenges as addictions. As long as I chase that feeling I want, I'm choosing to experience the opposite. The withdrawal is inevitable. If you want to be certain, you're choosing not only uncertainty but even more uncertainty than you experienced before.

The second loop is all about avoiding danger. When you react to an uncertainty, you're sending a loud message to your brain: "If this thing I'm worried about actually happened, it would be terrible! It's dangerous. I have to avoid it." Your brain likes to protect you from danger so it's helpfully going to look for all of the ways that dangerous thing might happen. If you worry about a friend posting embarrassing photos of you online after a night out, so you keep checking to see if he's posted anything, that tells your brain you're worried about what people will think about you. So your brain will start to look for other ways that you might get embarrassed: What if you stink? What if somebody accuses you of a crime you didn't commit? What if somebody is recording you naked in the bathroom and they're going to share the video online? And then you'll have to start checking to make sure all of those things aren't coming true.

When these two loops get spinning together, it's disastrous. But it doesn't happen instantly. Checking my water bottle that night wouldn't have sent me immediately spiraling down into a compulsive pit of despair. Getting these loops spun up is a practice, just as stopping them takes time and practice.

BUT WHAT IF MY COMPULSIONS DON'T BOTHER ME?

Most won't. It's entirely possible that they won't seem to interfere with your life. That doesn't mean they're not part of the problem. You might notice that checking on your kids constantly is affecting your life and theirs negatively, but all of the checking you do at work or in your relationship with your partner might seem useful. Compulsions are practices. Do you want to be skilled at them? Do you want to keep getting better at them until you notice that they're causing you distress?

We currently have this illness-first, mental health care system that's focused on symptoms and crises. You have to get sick to get help. We pretend that people who aren't in crisis don't have mental health issues to take care of. This is built into the systems governing how we approach mental health care. In the *Diagnostic and Statistical Manual of Mental Disorders 5*, the hefty tome published by the American Psychiatric Association providing criteria to diagnose mental illnesses, there's a clause in the diagnostic criteria for OCD that I call the distress clause. You can find this in the criteria for other disorders as well, such as bipolar disorder (twice), social anxiety disorder, and generalized anxiety disorder. There are variations in other disorders, too. The distress clause for OCD says that obsessions/compulsions must be time consuming or "cause clinically significant distress or impairment in social, occupational, or other important areas of functioning."

Imagine if we did this in other areas of health care, such as heart disease. Your doctor would see that your blood pressure is getting high, your cholesterol is in the danger zone, but you're not distressed by it, so what's the problem? It's not impairing your functioning. You like sitting all day! Keep eating the way you're eating. You love cheeseburgers! Keep not exercising the way you're not exercising. Drink all night! Come back when you're lying on the floor clutching your chest and then we can discuss healthier behaviors because you've become distressed and your functioning is presumably now impaired sufficiently to classify as "clinically significant."

You don't need to wait for a heart attack. You don't need to wait for a mental illness. Simply on practical terms, if you spend less time and energy reacting to uncertainty, you'll have more time to put into building and creating things you actually care about. Let your values guide you here. Something doesn't need to be "bad" or an "illness" to be something you kick out of your life. Is it helping you to be happy and healthy over the long term?

THE PRACTICE OF ELIMINATING A CHECKING COMPULSION

Some uncertainties are scarier than others. "What if I got an e-mail?" might not trigger as much anxiety in you as "What if my phone overheats while charging beside my bed and it causes a fire that kills me?"

I find that the ACT model of accepting the stuff in your head, choosing a direction aligned with your values, and then taking action is especially useful for dealing with uncertainties about frightening possibilities because by taking action while accepting that those fears are there, you show your brain that it doesn't need to be afraid. Similar to the coping compulsions example, I'll go through this using that ACT structure again and I'll add in two tricks that can help with overcoming terrifying uncertainties. We'll explore this using a common fear—that I might have left the stove on, it'll cause lots of damage, it might kill somebody, and I'll be blamed for it. Before we get into that, there are two things I want to explain:

1. Dealing with a compulsion like checking the stove is probably one you'll do further up your Hierarchy. Be honest with yourself about how difficult this might be. Build up your skills by tackling easier compulsions first. It took me significant work to cut out this compulsion.

2. I'm a fan of what's known as in vivo exposure. That involves living your life as you want to, which subsequently creates the opportunities for you to practice cutting out compulsions. To help with that, use the stove as you would like to use it. Don't avoid using the stove so you can reassure yourself that you don't need to check it. Of course, if you shrink your life, you have no anxieties to worry about. Don't do that. In the past, I avoided using the stove to make breakfast so that I wouldn't need to check the stove when I left in the morning. That's a compulsion. I love breakfasts. There are so many wonderful breakfasts I can make myself if I use the stove. So I started using the stove for breakfast every day. That created the uncertainty I could practice accepting without trying to use checking compulsions to get rid of.

Now let's dive into the practice of cutting out this compulsion:

I accept the stuff in my head and practice being present

- After using the stove for breakfast, I would get ready to leave. Inevitably, at that point, my brain would start to worry about whether I had turned off the stove. Not checking the stove would create an incredible amount of anxiety. I would physically feel terrible. I'd be irritable. I'd be on the verge of a panic attack. I would hear people shouting at me for burning down the apartment building. And I can accept all of that. It's okay for that uncertainty and subsequent anxiety to be there. That's an experience I can have in the present.

- When cutting out compulsions that cause significant anxiety, there are two different approaches that have helped me. In a little e-book called *The Acceptance Field Guide*, which I wrote early in my peer support career, I called these the Two Tricks. They might seem contradictory. Test them out. You may find they work in different situations, or on different days. Sometimes I would sit with the question about whether the stove was on. Other times I would accept the consequences. Both were useful to practice. Here's how they work:

TRICK #1—SIT WITH THE QUESTION.

Why do we answer the questions our brains throw at us? It was an incredible revelation the day I realized I didn't have to answer them. Why had nobody ever told me that?! It took about twenty-nine years to learn that I don't actually have to be certain about the uncertainties in my head. If my brain throws a ball, I don't have to chase it. I'm not a dog. If my brain is wondering if the stove is on, it can wonder that. Maybe it is on. Maybe it isn't. I don't have to answer. My brain doesn't know if the stove is on or if I turned it off! That uncertainty can be there. I can feel uncertain and carry it with me unresolved as I do the things I value.

TRICK #2—ACCEPT THE CONSEQUENCES.

This is basically the complete opposite of the first trick. It's by far my favorite recovery skill but it's not for beginners. It's possible I'll never be able to get fire insurance for my home after I share this with you, but here we go: Using the same powerful imagination I tried using to picture the stove being off, I would instead picture the stove covered in bottles of cleaning supplies and cooking oils, the dishrags piled on top of them, a greasy frying pan on a burner, and all of the burners bright red-hot. I'd picture flames licking up around the stove, lighting the cupboards on fire, the cleaning fluid bottles, campfire propane canisters that somehow got piled onto the counter beside the stove, and it all exploding in a massive fireball shooting out the apartment windows. Trying to figure out if I left the stove on was irrelevant because I was already responsible for setting the building on fire. It happened. I did it. And I would picture myself coming back to the apartment later to a crowd of crying people yelling at me as the police handcuffed me and took me away to jail. They'd blame me for setting the fire on purpose. My picture would be on the news all night. ARSON MURDERER APPREHENDED. I'd be in jail for years. My life would be ruined. Nobody would ever want to be near me again. I'd be alone and hated for the rest of my life.

- So I would apply one of those tricks, which would bring up even more thoughts and unpleasant emotions, and I can have all of those experiences.

I choose a direction aligned with my values

- After applying one of those tricks, I'm either sitting in a massive amount of uncertainty or I'm convinced my life is over and this is my last day of freedom. My values help pull me through that. If I've used the second trick and I believe I'm going to jail later for burning down my building, I can look to my values to understand how I want to spend my remaining hours in a way that's healthy, and in a way I can be happy about. I can't change the past and what I've done, but I can make sure my next steps are aligned with my values.

I take action

- I don't value engaging in compulsions and making my health worse. So I won't invent a reason to go back into the kitchen so that I can covertly check the stove. I'm not going to engage in mental compulsions to try remembering that I turned off the stove so that I can reassure myself. I do value going to school or going to work to do things I care about and to see people whom I care about. I value contributing to my community. I value taking care of my health.

- So whatever it was that I was leaving my home to go and do, I'm going to leave and do that. Because I'm not a rock, I can choose where I go. I'll intentionally invest my time and energy in what I value. I don't have to wait for something to push me around.

- Throughout the day, when my brain worries about what I've done, I can repeat these steps all over again and bring my focus back to the valued actions that I'm practicing.

TRUSTING YOUR MINDFULNESS PRACTICE

For me, in the past, safety meant worrying about something and then checking it. Worry was the prerequisite for safety.

I was so accustomed to practicing mindlessness that my mind was always in a different place when I was cooking, or ironing, or speaking, or driving, so it was totally natural that I'd be anxious about those things. I knew I hadn't paid attention. I didn't know what I'd done. I relied on anxiety to keep me safe. I would often discover that the door was unlocked, the stove was on, I'd made embarrassing mistakes in e-mails, I'd miscounted money, I'd almost cut myself with a knife, people noticed I was obviously not paying attention in a conversation. My avid devotion to mindlessness made checking a necessity for survival.

When you remove checking compulsions, you have to do things the first time. You have to be present. You choose not to rely on anxiety anymore.

Even when we practice mindfulness, it's not so that we remember turning off the stove and can reassure ourselves that we did it. It certainly hasn't improved my memory. But I practice mindfulness and I trust in my practice. I trust that when I was at the stove, I was at the stove. I was there cooking. I was there cleaning up. I don't have to remember it. I practice trusting myself and I show my brain that I trust myself.

When you're practicing the checking challenges for this step's exercise, consider how you can deepen your mindfulness practice as a proactive support for handling uncertainty. When checking is no longer an option, what needs to change in your life?

EXERCISE: Checking Challenges

The exercises I explain below are here to give you some extra practice to develop the skills to cut out the checking compulsions you've identified in your Hierarchy.

Send an e-mail without rereading it.
This is so much fun and oh-so-helpful with not losing hours in an e-mail black hole: send an e-mail without rereading it.

Be mindful when writing it because you won't be coming back to reread those sentences. One way to help yourself with this is to consider how your values translate into writing an e-mail. Before starting to write, pick two or three things you want to give to the recipient. Write aligned with what you want to give. And hit SEND before your brain knows what's happening! Accept whatever uncertainties pop into your head.

Don't check if people are looking at you.
I always wanted to check if people were looking at me. Then I'd judge what I thought they were thinking about me. As soon as there were people around me, it was like I wasn't in control of where I looked—I had to make eye contact with everybody. Mostly I wanted to do that because then I would tell myself that people were attracted to me (so I wasn't going to be alone forever). Thinking about what other people were thinking about me was a compulsion that consumed tremendous amounts of my time.

Even if you don't experience that in the same way I did, there might be something else you feel the urge to look at frequently. Practice feeling that urge but not looking, not checking whatever it is that you look at to relieve your uncertainty. Maybe it's checking social media accounts, checking the news, checking for damage to your vehicle, checking your bank account, or checking statistics. Accept that the urge is there. Accept whatever your brain throws at you. Maybe the most attractive person ever is looking at you and because you didn't return their smoldering gaze, you'll never hook up with them and never sail off into the sunset together and you'll end up alone in a dingy nursing home playing checkers by yourself in a corner.

Don't check your reflection.

Try not checking how you look when you feel the urge. Maybe there is something in your teeth. Maybe your hair is all wrong. Maybe you have stains down the front of your pants and people will assume you've been doing disgusting things in the washroom. Practice accepting whatever uncertainties come up when you don't react to those urges to check. What do they tell you about your fears? Try practicing the Two Tricks we looked at earlier. Sometimes you'll find it useful to sit with the uncertainty and not check. Other times you can practice accepting the extreme consequences of your worries.

DON'T MAKE ILLNESS THE PREREQUISITE FOR HEALTH

Understand your fears

In terms of what's helped me the most in recovery is understanding that all my mental health issues were interrelated.
Although on the surface they appeared as different themes, at
their roots I could break them down into a couple of ideas. It
was also very useful for me to understand that I have control
over the things that I want to do!

—DENIS

As you're clearing away your compulsions, you'll start to see an ugly
monster or two chewing away at you underneath them, like we talked
about back in the chapter on recognizing your problems. The massive
range of specific symptoms we think we're struggling with are the
superficial expressions of only a few underlying fears. Trying to deal
with each symptom as a separate issue is like cleaning up a massive
warehouse full of a million individual pieces of garbage. With each
piece you clean up, you uncover another one underneath. There's
always another anxiety, always another urge, always another compulsion, to replace the one you cleaned up. But when you recognize
these as patterns and you see the commonalities that link all of these
challenges together, it's as though the garbage were already collected

in a couple of enormous bags. You can take a big marker and write your fear on each bag. Here is all of the junk I collected in reaction to my fear of death. Here is a bagful of the hearts I smashed up while avoiding my fear of being alone. Here is a bagful of everything I hoarded because I was afraid I wouldn't have enough.

WHAT IF I GET POISONED?

One of the fears I struggled with was that somebody would try to poison me. At the gym, in particular, I wouldn't leave my water bottle unattended. If I forgot it someplace or even let it out of my sight temporarily, I'd get very anxious. When I found my bottle, I wouldn't drink out of it. I'd check it to see if it looked like it had been tampered with, I'd empty it, rinse it out, dry it with paper towels, and even then, I can remember times when I wouldn't use it again until I could wash it a few times.

Superficially, this was a paranoid fear that somebody was trying to hurt me. But underneath that was a fear of death. My brain was very imaginative when it came to thinking of ways I could die. I had many compulsions connected to the fear of death.

The traditional way of doing cognitive behavioral therapy would have focused on trying to help me see how unlikely or irrational it was to believe that somebody was trying to poison me. It would have been about labeling that thought as a "cognitive distortion" or a paranoid thought and then adding up evidence to see why it was unlikely. But I never found that approach helpful. I could always think of a reason why, as unlikely as it might be, the fear was possible. My brain was as skilled at debating as it was at inventing creative ways to die. And debating about whether a thought is irrational or rational misses the underlying fear: death. It doesn't matter what label we stick on the thought; it's simply a sign pointing at the real issue.

Getting over my compulsions around being poisoned was about accepting the superficial fear (somebody will poison or infect my water bottle) and then also accepting the consequences of that (dying), which is what I was actually afraid of. This is where the second trick that I explained in the previous step—of accepting consequences—comes in handy.

So I'd pick up the bottle, recognize that my brain was throwing out all of these thoughts about it being poisoned or infected, and take a drink from it. I wouldn't engage in any compulsions. My brain would freak out because I was going to die now. I would agree with that. I was about to die, painfully, missing out on everything I'd ever wanted to do in life, choking out my last breath all alone later that night on the floor of my apartment in a pile of regrets and vomit. However, since this would be my last workout, I was going to enjoy it. I'd appreciate everything my body does for me. I wouldn't check how I looked in the mirror or avoid any exercises because I was afraid of failing, getting injured, or looking stupid. I would stick to my values and give myself a great workout, enjoying my last few moments being able to use my body.

This is tough. It will make you sweat. Cutting out compulsions might seem very difficult because all of the fears or uncertainties you're reacting to are terrifying. They are the complete opposite of what you want in life. You don't want to lose your job, or have your relationship end, or see anything bad happen to your children, or lose all of your money, or be hated by everybody—I understand that. I know exactly how it feels to believe that you've just harmed somebody, or that you're about to die, or that you've ruined your relationship, or that you've done any number of horrible things your brain can imagine, and believe them completely, without a shred of doubt. There is, however, incredible power in showing your brain it doesn't need to be afraid of those experiences any longer. You can show your brain that those experiences, ones that you've invested so many hours and days in trying to prevent, can happen. Not only can they happen, they've already happened. They're in the past now. You're not a time traveler so you can't change the past. All you can do is be in the present. You can be yourself now. You can act according to your values. You can trust yourself to handle this.

YOUR BRAIN IS TRYING TO HELP YOU

Our brains are trying to help us prevent the experiences we want to avoid. If you're afraid of death, your brain will start looking for all of the different ways you could die. As you react to more and more of the ways your brain thinks you could die, your brain helpfully finds even more uncertainties about death for you to control. This very natural progression expands throughout your life until you're constantly obsessing and giving up all of your time and energy to preventing death. It's an unfortunate way to miss out on living.

I don't want to make a sweeping generalization, but . . . we're all going to die. You'll die. I'll die. Everybody you know will die. Everybody you don't know will die. This is a reality of life. Like jumping in a pool and getting wet; when we jump into life, we surely will experience death.

The previous steps might have sparked some thoughts about death. What if I don't check the door lock and somebody breaks in and kills me? What if I'm responsible for an accident that kills other people? What if this feeling in my chest actually is a heart attack and the doctor is totally wrong about it being a panic attack?!

When you're able to recognize what you're afraid of at a deeper level, you can be kind and understanding to your brain when it throws up another uncertainty. Your brain is trying to protect you. It's like a little child that doesn't want anything bad to happen to you. It can't understand why you're not doing compulsions anymore. If you've taught your brain to be very afraid of death, it's only natural that it's constantly worrying about things that might cause you to die.

Although it's important to cut out compulsions, until you learn how to practice accepting the fears at the roots of your compulsions, your brain will always find something new to latch on to. If you stop researching illness symptoms online, your brain might move on to obsessing about toxins in your food or finding the "right" vitamins. If you stop trying to reassure yourself that you're not a murderer, your brain might move on to obsessing about your sexuality, or whether you're a rapist, or something else that you feel is the exact opposite of who you are. If you stop trying to control your coworkers, you may notice yourself trying to control your girlfriend.

Use this next exercise to dig deep underneath your compulsions. Find those big uncertainties you're trying to avoid. You can use the skills we're exploring to accept those uncertainties and get comfortable with them. When you can do that, your brain can stop worrying about them.

EXERCISE: The Five Whys

When we dig into the fears that bother us, commonalities beneath seemingly disparate fears and uncertainties begin to emerge. The Five Whys is an exercise from the world of design and business that can help you dig under your fears and find those common roots. It can help you see why you're doing what you're doing. Here's how to do the exercise:

1. Pick one of your compulsions.

2. Ask yourself: Why would it be bad to stop doing that?

3. Then take your answer and ask yourself: Why would that be bad (or wrong, or unwanted, etc.)?

4. Answer that question and again ask yourself why that would be bad.

5. Repeat this question-and-answer process a total of five times and see where you land.

Here's an example of how this works:

Compulsion: Rereading messages from your partner or somebody you're dating

Q1) Why would it be bad to stop rereading those messages?

A1) Because then I couldn't be certain about what they truly mean.

Q2) Why would it be bad not to know what the messages truly mean?

A2) Because I have to know if that person is still into me or not.

Q3) Why would it be bad if you didn't know whether she is still interested in you?

A3) Because I'm not going to waste my time investing in a relationship if she's not interested in me.

Q4) Why wouldn't you want to invest in a relationship if it won't be reciprocated?

A4) Because I could be putting that effort into a relationship with the right person who I am going to spend the rest of my life with.

Q5) Why would it be bad to put everything into a relationship with the wrong person?

A5) Because I would feel so ripped off. I'd end up giving everything and then I'd be left there all alone while the person I should've been with will have gone off to be with somebody else.

Notice how we went from checking and rereading messages to something that's much more fundamental about how that person approaches relationships. His actions are all about avoiding things he's afraid of (being with the wrong person, losing the investment of his resources, being alone) instead of trying to create something he actually wants to experience. If he looked at other areas of his life, he'd probably see that he's taking a similarly transactional and fear-based approach in business relationships and friendships—always holding back, averse to risk, letting fear guide his actions, waiting for the other person to commit fully and give more. Although the compulsions around rereading messages might bother him the most, if he doesn't want these fears to continually pop up in the form of new compulsions, he can help himself by accepting more uncertainty and taking a more pro-active, values-based approach in all of his relationships.

*

As you do this exercise, modify the questions to fit the context and push into difficult subjects. You may need to go further than five questions. And keep an open mind. Many of the ways you see yourself reacting to those root fears or uncertainties in your everyday actions may not be things you've defined as compulsions. They may be ways of thinking and behaving that you feel are part of your personality. However, consider that they are all ways you cultivate and maintain that fear.

LIKE JUMPING IN A POOL AND GETTING WET; WHEN WE JUMP INTO LIFE, WE SURELY WILL EXPERIENCE DEATH.

Stop controlling

In the novel *The Trial* by Franz Kafka, there's a parable that a priest tells the main character, K., as a way of explaining a common delusion people possess about the Law. The parable goes something like this: A man, arriving at an open door—the entrance to the Law—is greeted by a frightening-looking guard standing beside the doorway. The man requests admittance to the Law but the guard tells him that he can't go through the door just yet, and if he tries to go through the door, the guard can't be responsible for the terrible things that might happen to the man. There are even more frightening guards ahead. The door is ajar but the man is not sure what's on the other side. He decides not to risk it. He'll wait until it's the right time to enter. So he waits. Sometimes the guard chats with him. The man gives up all of his possessions to bribe the guard for admittance to the Law but to no avail. The man grows very old waiting. Year after year, he sits by the door, hoping the right time to enter will soon arrive. And then, one day, the man, now very old and feeling that he's on the verge of death, notices a light flooding out from the doorway. He looks up at the guard. Surely this is a sign that the right time has finally come. He asks the guard if it's time. In answer to the man's last question, the guard explains that this particular door was meant only for that man and now that he's dying, the guard will shut the door. The man dies.

Best. Story. Ever.

What that man did at the door is a typical controlling compulsion: avoidance. He was uncertain about something bad happening and he tried to control that uncertainty by not taking the actions he actually wanted to take in life. He might have felt that he was avoiding suffering, but the result of that was a lifetime of suffering and he didn't go where he wanted to go.

THE NATURE OF CONTROLLING BEHAVIORS

Controlling compulsions are the actions we take to control everybody and everything around us, in the past and the future, to avoid uncertainty, anxiety, and other feelings we don't like. For example:

- A young man who restricts his food intake and exercises obsessively because he thinks the image he sees in the mirror looks wrong and he wants to "correct" it.

- A girl who lies about her age and posts flattering pictures from several years ago on her dating profile because she's afraid of not getting any messages.

- A manager who creates systems in her office that depend on every decision going through her so she can be certain nobody makes a mistake that will impact her performance review.

- A boy who turns his video game console off and on in a precise order and needs to play segments of a new game "cleanly," without any mistakes, to prevent his personality from being stolen.

- A woman who tries to control what her girlfriend does and where she goes because she's afraid she'll meet somebody better and leave her.

Of course, that young man will only see more and more things wrong in the mirror. That girl will experience even worse rejection when her dates discover she isn't the person she presented herself as on her profile. That manager's projects will fail because of the oversight bottlenecks she creates from fear of failure. That boy will need to play the game over and over again and he'll get so agitated about it that his parents will wonder what happened to their son. That woman will scare her girlfriend away.

The more you control, the more you must control. That is the nature of controlling. Only commit to it if you want more of the uncertainties you're trying to control.

But how do you stop trying to control the universe and everybody in it? Especially when you're trying to control the universe only to prevent terrible things from happening, like death.

THE PRACTICE OF ELIMINATING A CONTROLLING COMPULSION

Notice in this example as well how checking compulsions are tightly wound up with controlling compulsions. You'll often see that you experience uncertainty, you check, you judge what you check, that creates more uncertainty, and then you try to control that uncertainty.

We'll go through this example using the same ACT format as in the previous examples: accepting and being present with whatever is happening in your head, choosing a direction that you value, and then acting in a way that's aligned with your values.

In this example, I'll share how I practiced overcoming the fear that I was going to be poisoned:

I accept the stuff in my head and practice being present

- I would purposefully trigger the stuff in my head by leaving my bottle someplace while I went to get a towel from another part of the gym.

- When I'd return to pick up my bottle, my brain would start throwing up all of these thoughts about whether somebody might have touched the bottle or poisoned it. I was also anxious about contracting diseases, so the worries in my brain were always a mix of poisoning and whatever disease I was afraid of that week. I often referred to it as "HIVEbolaherpes." It's totally fine that I have those thoughts and feel anxious. I know my brain is reacting to my fear of death.

- I would agree with all of the thoughts that came up. I would use that second trick, of accepting the consequences: I would be poisoned the moment I took a drink out of my bottle. I would die later that day, slowly and painfully. Even if the poison didn't kill me, somebody had probably rubbed infected blood around the rim of my water bottle, and because I often bit the inside of my cheek while I had anxious dreams at night, the disease would get into my bloodstream. People would doubt my story about how I got the disease. Nobody would ever want to date me. I wouldn't get to accomplish any of the things I'd wanted to do in life.

I choose a direction aligned with my values

- I'd feel an intense urge to check if there was anything like blood on the bottle or anywhere around it. I would also feel the urge to check the people nearby to see if anybody looked suspicious. But I'm focused on actions, not obsessions, so I'm not going to engage in compulsions as a reaction to the obsessions. I'll choose to do something aligned with my values. I'm at the gym so how can I support my exercise practice? Because I'm about to die, how do I want to spend my last hours or my last day? I would consider what I can do that's aligned with who I am and what I care about. Spending my last day reacting to the stuff in my head is not something I value.

I take action

- It's important to be hydrated when working out, so I would unscrew the cap, take a drink out of it, making sure to touch my lips to the rim (that was something I often avoided doing in the past), and then I'd swallow and go straight to the next exercise without looking at the bottle.

- I would keep working out as intensely as I did before I poisoned myself. This is so important because it shows my brain that I'm not afraid. I'm indicating to my brain that it was wrong to bring up this anxiety. The labels I've attached to death and disease were incorrect. I don't have to react to death or disease with panic and avoidance. I can welcome them and do what I care about. If it's my last workout, I'd better have a great one. There's no point in saving up some energy for tomorrow or not doing squats because I'm afraid of hurting my knees. I can practice mindfulness and enjoy the movement of my body, the racing of my heart, a deep exhale as I push the weights, the sunlight shining through the windows, the music, all of the people around me sweating away, with their own anxieties, their own suffering, their own hopes for themselves and their families.

COMPLEX CONTROLLING COMPULSIONS

On one hand, accepting that I might get killed seems intense, but it's relatively simple—I accept that I will die and I do what I value. There are many instances where eliminating a controlling compulsion is emotionally intense but straightforward—you accept that you'll die, be hated, cause an accident, get fired, dumped, etc., and you do what you value. In many situations, however, like at work, in relationships, in society or politics, controlling is all we've ever known. We still want to reach our goals at work, we still want to have relationships, so how do we do that without controlling?

The second section of the book is all about making that shift away from your control addiction and toward a life of accepting uncertainty and doing what you value. We'll explore many exercises for achieving that. So for this exercise, you'll practice flexing your imagination in a way that can help you open up alternatives to the catastrophizing that fuels our need to control everything.

EXERCISE: Practicing Possibility

For years, in any situation, my mind would do something I called "going from A to Z to the end of the world." When presented with nearly any situation, real or imagined, I would immediately experience the worst possible outcome. I mentioned some examples of this in the first chapter, like when I would walk up steps and see myself falling, then feel my teeth get smashed in. Those types of experiences happened constantly. If I was walking across a grate on the sidewalk, I'd see it collapsing and me getting impaled on some rebar in a muddy hole, so I'd walk around it. If I thought about cooking a dish to take to a friend's dinner party, my mind would quickly imagine me chopping off my fingers while preparing the vegetables, so I would convince myself I should buy some takeout and say I was too busy to cook. At the gym, when I thought about picking up some weights off the floor, I'd hear somebody angrily yelling at me to put them back because they were using them, so I'd find an empty machine to use instead.

My brain did not know how to imagine anything else happening except the worst possible scenario. So I needed to give my brain the ability to imagine things going well. Like any mental ability, I needed to build that through practice. I needed to practice imagining myself handling challenges. At the same time, I also need to help my brain with cognitive defusion— recognizing that all of this stuff in my head was nothing more than stuff in my head. And I needed to approach all of this with the same dedication and passion I had devoted to years of obsessing about the end of the world. Here's how you do it:

How to Practice Possibility

1. **Live your life.** Do things you value. While you're doing that, your brain—being the helpful brain that it is—will throw up intrusive thoughts or images about terrible things happening that will interfere with what you want in life.

2. **When your brain throws up those intrusive thoughts or images, recognize that it's stuff in your head you're experiencing.** It's not you. This can be tricky at first, because in the past, possibly even now, you might have liked that you could always think of the things that could go wrong in any situation. You were the one who spotted the problems in the plans of others. You were the one who took care of your careless family.

3. **Imagine yourself overcoming challenges in the most amazingly fantastical ways.** I'll give you some examples of

what I mean: If you often worry about accidents when you're driving, the next time you notice your brain starting to worry about getting hit, you could picture yourself masterfully maneuvering around the potential danger like you're a trained stunt car driver in a movie, swerving and dodging and speeding out of danger.

If you're going on a vacation to a remote island and you're worried about getting sick or hurt, you might instead imagine yourself riding a dolphin to the island just in time to attend a parade in your honor with all of the most delicious foods you could ever eat. If you're worried about having a panic attack on the trip there, you might picture yourself leading everybody in the airplane cabin in a choreographed dance number, with the flight attendants doing cartwheels out on the wings while miniature unicorns prance up and down the aisles.

If you worry about loved ones getting hurt, your brain probably discovers many different ways to worry about that. For anything it comes up with, you can try imagining your loved one doing something truly astounding to overcome that challenge. You could picture your spouse dodging an attack and then crushing the attackers with mixed martial arts skills you didn't even know he possessed. You could see your kids flying out of harm's way and carrying all of their friends to safety with them. You could imagine a car swerving into your mother as she slowly crosses the street, but instead of her getting hurt by the car, on contact the vehicle shreds into a million pieces of paper that flutter away in the breeze.

*

That's all there is to Practicing Possibility. You're intentionally imagining things working out fantastically well. It's simple, but it might be totally novel for you. You're probably incredibly skilled at imagining horrible things happening. This is a simple practice for building the ability to imagine wonderful things happening. There's nothing wrong with imagining horrible things happening. Practicing Possibility is about developing capacity. You're making it possible for your brain to imagine things you couldn't before because you never practiced imagining them. When you can imagine wonderful things happening as easily as you can imagine horrible things happening, you give your brain options.

I want to emphasize the importance of adding that fantastical element. This is all stuff in our heads. When you imagine something horrible happening, you probably believe it. The thought doesn't seem separate from reality. This exercise of Practicing Possibility helps you show yourself that a totally positive fantasy can exist in your head as easily as a thoroughly negative fantasy. I can imagine myself getting hit by a car as easily as I can imagine myself doing a backflip over a car. They're all thoughts. They're real thoughts. They're not reality.

Doesn't this contradict the trick of accepting the terrible consequences?

You could say that. But it's like saying that pull-ups contradict push-ups. You're exercising different muscles. Both are useful. It's like we have different mind muscles. Exercise them all and you'll be capable of adapting to a variety of challenges.

I found that second trick, of accepting consequences, and this exercising of Practicing Possibility were particularly helpful with fears I had related to knives. I had to get over the fear of slicing off my fingers and the fear of hurting others. So if I worried about accidentally stabbing somebody, I would picture myself juggling butcher knives in the air and tossing them around people, doing somersaults over the kitchen table, and catching the knives in my teeth. If I was worried about slicing my fingers off, I might just agree with that and see myself without fingers and picture the consequences of that happening. It's all about going back to that fundamental emotional fitness exercise and finding what's difficult for my brain, and then pushing into it so I remove barriers that get in my way of being myself.

STEP 12

Tame the monster

As you cut out all of those compulsions and you dig down into your fears, you'll uncover the monster that's made up of all of your uncertainties, anxieties, urges, and other experiences you don't like. For some, the monster is tiny. For others, it's enormous. But we all have this monster, and the more we feed it compulsions, the bigger it gets. If you keep feeding it, some parts of your life become off-limits. The monster can get so big that it squeezes you out of your favorite places and activities. It can do nasty things in our lives and leave its stench lingering in our memories.

It's especially difficult to care for a monster like this when you're at work. You might have tried to hide your monster. Maybe you shoved it under your desk so you could keep feeding it and hope nobody noticed. But that only allowed the monster to grow. It became more difficult to pretend that there wasn't a monster following you around to project meetings, shitting on your work, and stinking up the office.

Now that anxious, uncertain, fearful urge monster will try to scare you back into the way you did things before. It will threaten to mess up your relationships, ruin your family holidays, and get you fired from your job. But you don't have to get rid of it. Fighting it will only make it hungrier and angrier and it'll eat you. You can learn how to tame it.

EXPECT THE MONSTER TO PLAY TRICKS ON YOU

When you eliminate compulsions from your life, it's not uncommon to experience physical discomfort like headaches, exhaustion, indigestion, ringing in your ears, and whatever else that monster can throw at you to get you anxiously back into compulsions.

In the moments when I would feel an urge to engage in a compulsion and I would choose not to do it, it felt like my brain was shriveling up inside my head. It was a tingly, painful sensation, like slowly pulling Band-Aids off the inside of my skull.

When I was cutting out online compulsions, choosing not to engage in them would make me fall asleep. I can remember when I was practicing not using my computer and I would turn it off, pick up a brand-new book I'd purchased specifically for this week of cutting out online compulsions, and then the next thing I knew, I'd be waking up at four a.m. with all of the lights on, having totally passed out on the sofa early in the evening the moment I tried to read. That went on for about a week until the urge to engage in the compulsion subsided. Change was physically difficult for my brain and I had to make space in my life for that. Weird things will happen.

The monster will come up with reasons why these uncertainties and feelings you're experiencing are different, why you can actually get hurt this time, why you can finally solve this for good and it'll never come back if you just do this one compulsion!

Whatever tricks the monster tries to play on you, apply the skills we've been exploring. You can be mindful of the experience and welcome it with curiosity. You don't have to judge it. Don't get caught up in trying to escape the superficial symptoms—it's still the same monster. You don't have to let it push you back into old compulsions or new ones that feel necessary and "normal." You can stick to your values as you ride up and over that Unhappiness Curve. As you do that and be yourself, you'll grow larger than the monster and it'll become easier to wrap your arms around it and give it a hug.

YOU ARE NOT YOUR MONSTER (OR YOUR FARTS)

One challenge to taming the monster is that we conflate our identities with our monsters. It's something we learn to do. It's even built into our languages. In English, we say things like "I'm anxious," or "I need a shot of whiskey," or "I'm afraid." We don't see anxiety or craving or fear as things we experience or as the by-products of organs. Anxiety is nothing more than brain indigestion, but you would never say, "I'm indigestion." It's something you experience. You are not your farts. But for some reason, we often believe we are our thoughts, urges, fears, and anxieties. Conflating your self with the stuff in your head is what's known as cognitive fusion.

Cognitive defusion is an acceptance and commitment therapy skill that's about recognizing that the stuff in your head is stuff you experience. It's not you. Developing your cognitive defusion skills will help create space between you and the stuff in your head. With practice, you learn to experience whatever the monster spits out and give yourself the space to make a choice about what you want to do with that stuff, if you want to do anything at all with it.

Regular mindfulness and meditation practice will help you work on recognizing that you experience thoughts, feelings, or sensations. The previous exercise we looked at, Practicing Possibility, is also great for working on cognitive defusion. You get to show your brain how disconnected your thoughts are from reality. The exercise at the end of this step is a variation of a popular ACT exercise that will also help with working on this skill.

In the past, you might have experienced a fear charging into your mind and knocking you backward, or an urge that would yank you forward, flat on your face. By developing your cognitive defusion skills, you can recognize that you've run into an urge or a fear. You can see them for what they are; you can steady yourself and not get knocked over by them. Then, recognizing that they're not you—they're experiences—you can make a choice about the next step that's actually aligned with your values. You can experience that fear, accept that it's a real fear, but take a step toward it. Or you might notice an urge, accept that it's there, and decide that it is something you want to do, but in an hour or so.

The monster's attempts to push us back into compulsions become experiences that we sense as we take our journey through life. When we no longer conflate those with our selves, they're no longer threatening. We see that the monster can't hurt us. In fact, we can sit right on top of the monster and make it carry us around. The uncertainties and anxieties and other feelings we don't like that the monster spits out become part of the scenery, like clouds floating in the sky.

THOUGHTS ARE LIKE CLOUDS

Cognitive fusion isn't focused only on ourselves. We fuse the stuff in our heads with other people, practices, and objects. We say things like "That's disgusting," "Those people are dangerous," "He's wrong," "She's a slut," and so on. This practice is core to racism, sexism, bigotry, and violence. It's very hurtful to ourselves and others. You're using that same skill when you label a thought as something you need to solve, or you judge an experience as something you need to be certain about. You then become very focused on giving all of your time and energy to getting rid of those experiences you don't like.

One of the most common questions that come up in the Everybody Has a Brain online community is about how to stop reacting to these bad thoughts, images, and memories. When people are struggling to stop thinking about something or stop having some type of reaction, they're struggling with cognitive fusion. Thoughts, urges, images, or feelings keep popping up in their heads and they want to do something about them because they're afraid they'll ruin a special event coming up, or they're worried it means they're a monstrous person, or it's taking time away from the studying they need to do to graduate from school. When they have these experiences, they immediately and consistently give those experiences their attention and energy.

When this issue comes up, the question I often suggest that people consider is this: Why don't you spend all day thinking about bad clouds?

First of all, you've probably never labeled a cloud as "bad." Understand that judgment plays a major role in any struggle with thoughts or feelings. You can choose to label a thought or a feeling as bad in the same way you can label a cloud as bad.

Cognitive fusion is like attaching a judgment to a cloud and then putting that cloud in charge of your life. If you did that, you'd be constantly checking for bad clouds, and when one appeared, you'd immediately give it all of your time and energy. That cloud in the sky would control your mood. You'd believe it means things about you. You'd do everything you could think of to get rid of it. But the more you kept your attention on that bad cloud, the more you'd notice other nasty clouds around it, and your entire day would get consumed by clouds. You'd become so focused on trying to control the clouds you hate that it would be like standing in a fog, unable to look past the clouds you hate so much.

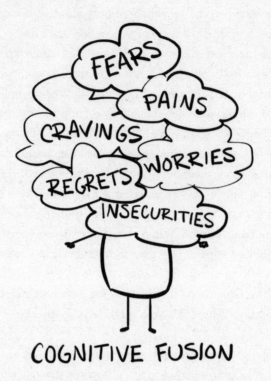

COGNITIVE FUSION

Cognitive defusion is like standing on the earth, present to everything in your life, with the clouds floating high over your head. You can pay attention to the clouds if you want to, or you can choose to give your awareness to anything else—the cars driving by, the voice of your hairdresser, the snow crunching under your boots, the sandwich you're making, the friend who's sharing a difficult secret with you. All of your experiences have equal importance and you can intentionally choose where to direct your attention.

COGNITIVE DEFUSION

SO I JUST IGNORE THE THOUGHTS?

Not exactly. Go back to that question I asked about bad clouds. Do you spend all day telling yourself to ignore clouds? If you woke up in the morning and you really wanted not to think about clouds because you've been focusing so much on them lately, you could decide not to look outside, not to watch the weather forecast, to wear a wide-brimmed hat outside so that you don't accidentally see any clouds, and you could avoid all small talk to prevent anybody mentioning that it's a cloudy day. No cloud triggers for you!

But what have you placed completely in charge of your life? The clouds. If you want to ignore something, you give that thing incredible power over your life.

With the exception of meteorologists and fishermen, most people practice "cloud defusion" every day. The clouds are there. You're aware of them. If you want to pay attention to them, you can. But you probably don't invest in actively trying to ignore the clouds. There's nothing wrong with seeing the clouds and acknowledging their existence. It doesn't mean anything about you. You don't have to do something about the clouds if you notice them. Cognitive defusion is about bringing the same practice to your thoughts. The clouds are simply part of the context in which you function.

That IF X THEN Y pattern is at work again when you're afraid that seeing a cloud in the sky means you're going to have a bad day, or that having a monster in your head means you're a monstrous person, or whatever conclusions you're drawing about unwanted experiences you're having. When we believe in that pattern, we try to avoid and ignore X because we think that X must mean Y. That's why it's important to break the pattern. If there's a cloud in the sky, there's a cloud in the sky. That's all. You can have that experience and choose to do things you value. If there's a monster in your head, there's a monster in your head. That's all.

But this takes practice. And what better way to practice than to take all of your intrusive thoughts and urges and anxieties and pack them into a car with you and drive them around town? With the next exercise, that's exactly what you'll get to do.

EXERCISE: Annoying Kids in a Car

It's tough to get up and over the Unhappiness Curve. You'll experience increased levels of anxiety, your brain will try to convince you that you're about to die, the voices in your head will tell you how worthless and incapable you are in very real, meticulously rational arguments, you'll have thoughts about terrible things happening to those you love, and it'll seem like the physical feelings you hate will not only get worse but never go away. It's a perfect time to take a road trip (with all of that stuff in your head that you hate).

The exercise I'll share with you here is a way to apply a popular acceptance and commitment therapy metaphor. Steven Hayes and Spencer Smith describe it in *Get Out of Your Mind and Into Your Life* as passengers on a bus. In Russ Harris's book *The Happiness Trap*—another great book using ACT techniques I'd recommend checking out—he describes a similar metaphor as demons on a boat. Personally, I find it useful to approach my brain as though it were a bunch of annoying children I'm driving around. Kids are always trying to get cookies, they have no grasp of reality, they make stuff up, they don't want to do healthy things, and they cry and whine all of the time for no reason, just like my brain. So I call this the Annoying Kids in a Car exercise. You'll need to drive these screaming toddlers up and over the Unhappiness Curve. Here's how this exercise works:

1. Grab a comfortable seat and close your eyes.

2. Picture yourself driving a car or some other vehicle that you like. Make it a vehicle that reflects your personality in some way. But make sure it has a backseat or two, because . . .

3. You're babysitting a bunch of rambunctious toddlers today. As you're driving, imagine the vehicle filling up with little kids shouting and screaming about the thoughts and feelings and urges with which you're struggling right now.

4. Hear the little girl screaming that she hates you because you're not good enough, the little boy crying in shock because you could fail, you could get hurt so badly. Hear the

child whining about wanting more cookies. Hear the little kid's panicked shouts about needing to stop and to turn around because you have to go back and deal with the past. Whatever it is that's difficult as you're climbing the Unhappiness Curve, imagine that as a little kid in the car with you. Hear it aloud from a little brat.

5. As you're imagining this experience, consider what you value. Yes, there is a bunch of screaming rascals in the backseat, but you have places to go. Punch that valued direction into your GPS and keep driving. Imagine the environment around you. What landmarks do you see that help you accept the shouts in the backseat and stay focused on where you're going? You can take these toddlers with you as you drive toward your values. If you react to everything a toddler shouts at you, you'll never get anywhere.

6. Remember that these compulsion urchins are clever. If they see you reacting to them, they'll push you even more. You can't reason with them—they believe in the Easter bunny and the tooth fairy. You can't forcibly try to control them—you might succeed but that'll only trap you in prison. They know you can't do anything to them. But they also can't do anything to you.

7. Try to see that these kids are scared, tired, and hurt. Can you hear them and feel compassion toward them? How would you treat a child who was crying and upset? Can you understand that the things they yell about come from a place of not being able to express clearly the pain they feel? Can you let them cry and shout? Maybe that's what they need to do right now.

8. Keep driving until you've had a good mental workout of noticing when you're distracted by the angry toddlers and then bringing your awareness back to your values and where you're going.

This is a practice that you can bring into your everyday life. Whenever my brain starts catastrophizing or throwing anxieties at me or whining about needing to do some compulsion, I can always hear that as an angry toddler crying. I can always express compassion to that voice or that image in my head. I know my brain is expressing that from a place of fear, but it can trust me. I'm going to help it do something that I know is healthy for both of us.

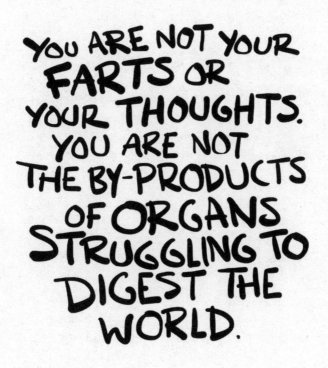

YOU ARE NOT YOUR FARTS OR YOUR THOUGHTS. YOU ARE NOT THE BY-PRODUCTS OF ORGANS STRUGGLING TO DIGEST THE WORLD.

PART TWO

The Transformation

Switch the fuel for life from fear to values

As you become more skilled at taming the monster and you stop feeding it compulsions, you'll notice the monster doesn't hang around you so much anymore. Even when it does show up to beg for compulsions, you don't spend your time feeding it. But you'll notice how much you depended on the monster to give you purpose in life. Now you won't have all of that fear and anxiety fueling your actions. This presents its own challenges.

Life without anxiety is terrifying. I remember very clearly the first time I noticed I wasn't anxious about anything—it was one of the scariest experiences of my life.

One morning, several months after I'd finished with my therapists and continued cutting out compulsions on my own, I was walking down the path behind my apartment building, on my way to a class at grad school. The sun shone through the leaves of the trees along the path and lit it up in this soft green glow. The temperature was perfect. It was beautiful. And then a worry popped into my head about people discovering I'd spent my morning on compulsions.

But I hadn't. I hadn't gone back to check anything. I hadn't done any rituals before I left. I hadn't spent the morning on my computer and then rushed to get ready at the last second.

I was on my way to a class, there would be a group of people there, and I had nothing to hide from them. I wasn't ashamed of anything. I wasn't worrying about the past or the future.

I began to tingle all over. The waves of a full-body panic attack started flowing out of every cell in my body. Nothing to worry about meant not having any uncertainties to control.

I had always functioned by reacting to uncertainty and then feeling good about preventing my fears from coming true. I depended on the monster spewing out uncertainties and anxieties and feelings I didn't like in order to have direction in life. I washed, I ate, I exercised, I socialized, I worked, I studied, I dated, I did everything imaginable as a reaction to whatever the anxiety monster vomited and shit into my life. I lived only to react. I didn't know how to function without constantly fixing problems.

Without the monster to feed, I had to find a new way to function. If I wanted to build better mental health and, most important, sustain it, I had to get an entirely new fuel for even the most basic activities in life. That fuel is my values.

So in this second section of the book, we're going to explore how to succeed with transforming your life from one that's a reaction to fear and anxiety to one that's proactively fueled by your values. This section is all about how to live with you in charge of your life instead of the monster.

EVERYTHING IS MENTAL HEALTH

Be holistic about your mental health. By "holistic" I don't mean light some candles and sprinkle lavender oil around. I mean see the whole system and make changes throughout it. How you work, how you study, how you communicate, how you exercise, how you eat, how you sleep—how you do everything is connected to your mental health.

If you focus on only a few compulsions or situations in which you struggle with emotions you don't like, you are the guy who goes into the gym to do only exercises for his biceps and spends most of the time trying to find the right angle in the mirrors to snap a picture of himself flexing so he can post it online, #curlsforthegirls.

Getting holistic is about practicing acceptance with uncertainty throughout your life. If you're somebody, for instance, who experiences a lot of anxiety in relationships because you struggle with uncertainty about whether your partner truly loves you and whether you're good enough for her and whether you're better than her previous partners, that might be the uncertainty you most want to learn how to handle. That's not independent of how you handle uncertainty throughout your life. Every time you experience uncertainty about health, or finances, or work, or your appearance, you'll have an opportunity to make changes with how you accept those uncertainties. Like we discussed in the step on checking compulsions, making changes in those other areas to accept uncertainty and align your actions with your values will help you accept the uncertainties you're experiencing in your relationship.

The values that you set earlier in the book will be your compass. They can help guide you in any situation. When you approach life from a values-based approach and ask the right kinds of questions—How can I do what I value in this situation? How can I do things that make me healthy and happy over the long term? How can I contribute to my community in a way that's healthy for me and my community over the long term?—then it becomes very necessary to look at everything on an ongoing basis. You're not solving a problem, you're creating your life. That's something you can do in every moment. How will you act as yourself, in a way that aligns with your values, throughout all of the systems in your life?

I'll explore a few examples below of the types of changes you might make throughout your life as you switch from a reactive, fear-based approach to a proactive, values-based approach:

Work/School/Life Balance

There is only life. Wherever you're breathing, that's your life. The concept of work/life balance is absurd. Your life won't start after you finish school, after you find the right person, after you're done working for the day, after you make enough money, after whatever you think is just over the horizon. Your life is right now. It's everything you do. It's every minute of today. So your values matter wherever you're doing whatever you do. That's your life.

Take some time to consider how your values translate into specific actions at work or at school. The culture around you might be highly focused on compulsions. It might encourage them. Be aware of that. How will you navigate that environment? Instead of reacting to the fear of being fired or the fear of being disliked or the fear of being responsible for a mistake, how can you work proactively to build and create what matters to you?

One way you'll likely find that a values-based approach manifests itself in your work is in the ability to say no. When you react to fear, it's easy to take on more work than you can do because you're afraid of saying no to a colleague or your boss. Or you might agree to act in a way that isn't aligned with your values because you don't see anybody else refusing to do it. You're afraid of what people will say about you if you refuse. Acting according to your values is about standing up for what you believe in. When you make decisions based on your values, the opportunities to say no and the benefits of doing that become much clearer. You're practicing being yourself. It's okay if your fears come true because you're building something stronger and more fulfilling.

Your values can't be something you set aside in your professional life and then hope to use in the few hours when you're not working or studying. Your practice is wherever you're breathing.

Social Media

How you use social media and the Internet in general can either be a way to practice your values or be all about practicing misery and encouraging your brain to give you even more uncertainties and urges to chase after.

It shouldn't be surprising that we can make our mental health worse online. Imagine if you engaged in the same behaviors you engage in online in the real world—you went around in your underwear to all of your friends each day to ask them if they liked how you look, spent hours each week stalking a model and judging yourself for not being as muscular as he is, ran around listening to conversations, and shouted abuse at anybody you disagreed with.

If you did those things in real life, I don't think anybody would be surprised if you ended up a miserable, anxious wreck. You'd probably get thrown in jail, too. It's no wonder that people question if there's a link between social media and poor mental health. But it's not social media that's the problem. It's what you do on it that's the problem.

As you make the switch to a values-fueled life, you're probably going to make big changes in how and what you do. How will your values translate into your actions online?

One of the biggest shifts you might make is from getting to giving. If you go online to get likes, reassurance, or relief, that's all about taking—trying to get stuff. You'll find it more fulfilling to practice giving. How do you give support to your friends or to strangers? How do you make others feel happy or lucky? How can you give people useful information?

When you make the shift from getting to giving, you bring success close to you. When you're done giving what you came to give, you can go and do something else. You've acted in line with your values and you're done. When you go online to get things, social media becomes a bottomless pit. You'll dig forever in search of what you're lacking.

Clothes and Grooming

This can be one of the trickiest values to change because we're bombarded by messages that we dress ourselves and take care of our appearance only to control what others think about us, to avoid embarrassment, to look sexy, to avoid exclusion. But that's guaranteed to make you anxious (and buy more clothes and more makeup, which is why we're fed those messages). Shifting from that approach to one that is based on caring for your appearance as an expression of yourself is liberating. You might think that not focusing on what others think about how you look would lead to you not taking care of yourself, but you'll discover that you'll take much better care of yourself.

When I cared about myself only as a means to control what others thought about me, if I didn't plan on seeing anybody that day or I wasn't looking to date anybody, my appearance and self-care would quickly go downhill. How I dressed, groomed, and cleaned was entirely fueled by anxiety. Don't get stuck in that trap. Identify how you want to care for yourself (for you) and stick with that. If there are particular activities you enjoy doing to care for your body, make them part of your Awesome Schedule.

When you get dressed in the morning, watch out for turning that into rumination practice time. Can you get dressed as an expression of yourself, not as an attempt to avoid fears or control other people? When you're shaving, washing, or doing any one of the millions of grooming activities we do, can you make that about caring for yourself and appreciating your body instead of trying to solve problems or fight smells or hate being human? This is an opportunity to practice appreciating yourself and showing your brain that your values don't fluctuate based on what you think others think about you.

Relationships

Romantic relationships are all about navigating uncertainty. Instead of asking somebody out on a date, it'd be more appropriate to ask if she'd like to join in a throuple with you and a hot, steamy mess of uncertainty. You can hold hands while experiencing life's wondrous unknowables together.

Craving certainty in a relationship and trying to control yourself or manipulate your partner as a reaction to uncertainty can quickly break apart a relationship.

You can't know for certain if your partner loves you, or whether he's the right person for you, or whether this relationship will last. What you can know is whether you're giving to the relationship, in this moment, in a way that aligns with your values. Take time individually, and with your partner, to articulate what matters to each of you in a relationship. What are the values of your relationship? How does each of your individual values translate into shared actions? Then put your time and energy into building that relationship.

Shifting the focus to values can also help with getting out of bad relationships, especially if we're staying in those bad relationships because we're afraid of what could happen if we leave. If we're reacting to the fear of being alone, or unloved, or not valued, or the fear of hurting somebody, it's easy to make decisions in reaction to those fears that cause only more pain for ourselves, as with any compulsion. But if you're looking at whether you can build a relationship with this person in a way that's aligned with your values, then the conversation is much different.

Cleaning

When I'm talking about cleaning here, I mean it in all forms—cleaning yourself, objects, rooms, whatever. Most of us spend a significant amount of time cleaning. You can make that time an opportunity to practice building better mental health or you can make it an opportunity to practice fear.

Compulsive cleaning is a stereotypical OCD symptom, but I didn't start doing it until my mental health challenges were relatively severe.

I became very focused on hand washing. I'd wash my hands and then a few minutes later question if I'd washed them well enough or washed them at all, then go back and wash them again. If I touched things I thought might be "contaminated," I had to wash my hands quickly before touching anything else. I would also wash my hands under scalding hot water because I wanted to feel the pain so I could be certain I'd killed off all of the flesh-eating bacteria or Ebola or whatever it was that I was afraid of that day. I didn't want to spread that contamination to others and be responsible for hurting them. You can see that IF X THEN Y pattern at work there again: IF X (my hands aren't in pain) THEN Y (they're not clean and I need to clean them again) and IF X (I'm not perfectly clean) THEN Y (I'll spread a disease to others and kill them and everybody will hate me).

In a subtler way, that IF X THEN Y pattern was at work whenever I cleaned my home because I cleaned only as a reaction to the fear of being judged by others. That might seem normal, but that's the type of normal practice that trains the brain to be constantly worrying and afraid. If I clean only when I'm afraid or anxious, it makes anxiety necessary for action. That's not a useful approach to choose if you don't like anxiety.

Whether it's hand washing or cleaning your home, do it for you and do it proactively because it's an action you value. Revisit the values you articulated earlier and see if caring for yourself or your home fit in there somewhere. If not, you might want to add in a value. You don't have to wash your hands because you're trying to control the future. You can wash your hands as a way of appreciating your body. You don't have to clean your kitchen as an attempt to control the thoughts of others. You can clean your kitchen because you're grateful for the help it provides you, or simply because it's a thing you do.

As you wash and clean, it's an opportunity to incorporate your mindfulness skills into your daily life. Keep your mind with you and open up your awareness to your senses—the smell of the soap, the motion of your hands as you wipe the counter, the shine of a clean stove top—all in the present.

DON'T GO BACK TO NORMAL

When somebody says "I know it's just the bipolar talking when I want to find a hookup," or "I can usually tell when it's a delusional thought," or "My anxiety is about social situations," it misses the much broader role that mental health plays in her life. Our mental health challenges are more than the specific problems we see poking up out of the fog of our everyday lives. Yes, there are particular symptoms that you can judge and label, but those are like the peaks in a mountain range. Label them, plant your flag on them if you want to, but remember that the peaks are held up by much larger foundations. If the Himalayas are in your way, knocking the top off of Mount Everest to make it a more normal-size mountain removes only a label. You still have a massive wall of rock in your way. Your unique and noticeable symptoms rest on a foundation of totally average, normal practices.

People often tell me they "just want to be normal again," they want to "go back to the way it was when things were normal." And I cannot emphasize enough how important it is not to go back to the way things were. Do not go back to what you thought of as "normal." Normal got you here. Remember that guy from step 6 who kept jumping in the pool and hated being wet? Don't be that guy.

I don't recommend normal to anyone. It's just like with physical fitness—there might have been a time when you could have eaten whatever you wanted and drank whatever you wanted and you didn't have to exercise and everything worked fine and it was no problem. That was normal. And that practice, over the years, very naturally leads to being out of shape. With mental health, you may have spent many years engaging in compulsions and believed that they "worked." They did provide short-term relief. You loved feeling certain. Your anxiety monster was cute and quirky. You could take it everywhere. You could joke about it! I totally get that. Looking back now, I can see that I was working my way up to a mental illness from a very young age. One of my earliest memories that I can recall clearly is from a week I spent one summer constantly ruminating about whether I'd damaged some furniture at a friend's house. From the moment I woke up until I went to bed, that's all I thought about, for days. Every time the phone rang, I was sure it was this kid's parents calling my parents to report what I'd done. Every time I saw that kid, I was checking to see if he was angry with me. What if he'd been punished for what I'd done?! He would hate me forever (although I'd be relieved that he got punished instead of me).

For decades, my normal was nothing but coping, checking, and controlling compulsions. Among all of my other compulsions, I continued with that practice of spending entire weeks worrying about horrible things I thought I'd done. I became very skilled at doing all of that "normal" stuff while also doing well in school, getting good jobs, and developing great friendships. I thought my normal worked incredibly well and I had the rewards from society to prove that my normal was perfectly fine. It was not.

Struggling with mental health is normal. When charities are doing mental health awareness campaigns, they like to talk about research that shows that one in five people will experience a mental illness in a given year. But that's only the number of people around you right now struggling with a diagnosable mental illness. The lifetime prevalence is much higher. A study published in 2005 that did face-to-face interviews with more than nine thousand people estimated the lifetime prevalence of experiencing a mental illness at 46.4 percent. That's nearly half the population. It doesn't get much more normal than that. And it's not like the other 54 percent of the population has perfect mental health.

Normal people don't have great mental health, just like normal people don't have great physical health. Struggling with physical health is normal. If somebody is in great physical shape, it's likely they do not do the same things that the average person does. They do not act normal. And if you don't want to go back to struggling with your mental health, I don't suggest you pursue normal, either.

If any of the changes I've mentioned so far don't sound normal to you, well, you're damn right they're not normal.

BUT IF WE DON'T REACT TO FEAR, WON'T EVERYBODY JUST DO WHATEVER THEY WANT?

The premise of this worry is essentially that we'll all become bank robbers and murderers the moment we overcome our fears because only the fear of punishment or guilt is holding us back from killing whoever keeps stealing lunches from the office fridge.

You may have many anxieties about doing terrible things or being judged by others and you may believe that your fear of doing those things is actually good for you and helps you. Through improving your mental health, you can learn to experience incredible amounts of anxiety, to immerse yourself in the depths of guilt, to overcome your fear of death, and all manner of feats of emotional awesomeness without those experiences controlling your actions. Fear will no longer trap you in a limiting cage. It will no longer decide where you can go and what you can do.

With that freedom comes responsibility. You can practice trusting yourself with that responsibility. This is why it's so important to let your values fuel your actions. Feel empowered by that opportunity. You can proactively make choices for yourself and those around you, not out of fear but because you want to live. You don't need fear to control you. This may be difficult to imagine right now but our natural inclination, when fear is not in control, is to do good.

When I spoke with Dr. Steven Hayes while I was writing this book, we talked about this topic and he told me that when people are "healthy and whole, it turns out, they want to create and help others. They want to live and love. They want to dance and contribute and plant and eat and create and grow and change."

It is so true. I hope you get to do all of that and so much more.

STICKING TO VALUES IS DIFFICULT BUT MENTAL ILLNESS IS MORE DIFFICULT

Switching to values is challenging. You'll catch yourself doing things you don't value all of the time. You'll end up lying on your bed, holding your phone in front of your nose, watching cat videos for hours, and then suddenly realize you've lost the entire morning to staring at moving lights again. That's normal.

When you catch yourself mindlessly flipping through websites on your phone, recognize that it's happening. You can make a choice about how you want to spend your time.

I love writing and doing creative things in my free time. In the past I would say I didn't have enough time to do what I loved and I'd get upset about that. I'd get very agitated if anybody interfered with my time. I was terrified of dying before accomplishing all of the things I wanted to do. But I had lots of time. I simply spent it on things that didn't matter to me. Now I can recognize when I'm starting to put time into things I don't value and I can choose to put my time into things I do value. I can choose to spend that time with people I care about or to learn how to cook something healthy for dinner.

This is an extension of our mindfulness practice. We notice when we've wandered off to do things we don't value and then we come back to our practice. Ronit Jinich has often reminded me during a meditation session that "returning is the practice." Your values will help you return to the path in your own life.

A big support in returning to an action that's aligned with your values is knowing what those actions are and knowing how you can engage in everyday actions in a way that's not dependent on anxiety. This next exercise will help you with articulating those actions.

EXERCISE: The Switch List

This exercise is all about understanding how you can switch from a fear-based approach to a values-based approach with everyday activities. Apply everything you've learned in the book so far to making these changes: you're going to let yourself experience feelings, you're not going to engage in compulsions, you're going to act proactively instead of reactively, you're going to act in line with your values.

1. Grab a piece of paper and draw a line down the middle. At the top of the paper on the left-hand side, write "Fear-based." At the top of the paper on the right-hand side of the line, write "Values-based."

2. In the "Fear-based" column, write some of the compulsions you engage in as a reaction to various fears. List compulsions that involve behaviors you'll keep in your life. There are some examples in a table after these instructions if you need some suggestions.

3. In the "Values-based" column, write how you'll do that same action but reframe it so that it's proactively helping you move toward what you value.

4. Put these changes into action using tools we've already explored. You can add them into your Hierarchy, for instance. You might pick a week coming up as the week you'll challenge yourself to open your e-mail only when you

have an e-mail to send. Or there might be specific activities
you can incorporate into your Awesome Schedule. Perhaps
in the past you exercised only because the summer was
coming, but now you'll make exercise a regular part of your
life, not dependent on reacting to the fear of impending
public disrobement.

Here are some more examples of making the switch from fear-
based actions to values-based actions:

FEAR-BASED		VALUES-BASED
Dieting because I hate how I look	→	Eating to fuel my running practice
Moving to a new city to avoid all of the memories that the one I live in triggers and because "I just want to get away from it all"	→	Living in a place that's optimal for doing things I value in life
Sending messages to my partner to get a quick response so I know she cares about me	→	Sending messages to express to my partner how much I care about her
Cleaning my home because I'm afraid of getting judged by visitors	→	Cleaning my home because I care about the place in which I live
Getting something on my résumé because I'm afraid people won't respect me if I don't have the right title or degree	→	Doing things that add value to my community or my profession
Showering to avoid feeling contaminated	→	Showering to care for and appreciate my body
Helping a customer because I'll get fired if I don't	→	Helping a customer because I want to support people in the same way I like to be supported
Avoiding my friends because I don't feel like myself today	→	Spending time with my friends because that's an action that reflects my values

FEAR-BASED		VALUES-BASED
Posting a comment online to correct somebody I believe is wrong	→	Creating something of use to people and posting that online
Meditating as an attempt to escape feelings I don't like	→	Meditating to practice accepting totally natural human experiences

IN ANY MOMENT YOU CAN RETURN TO THE PRACTICE OF BEING YOURSELF

Break your motivation addiction

I'll admit it, you have a lot of work to do. You've started meditating, eliminating the compulsions in your life, doing more of the things you actually care about, letting yourself have feelings you've avoided for years, and making changes at work, in relationships, in how you use the Internet, in how you eat, in how you exercise—and we're not even done yet. I know there's more work coming up in the steps ahead (because I put it there). Building better mental health takes work, like building better physical health. So you might be wondering how you'll get motivated to make all of the changes we've explored.

My recommendation: don't.

MOTIVATION IS A UNICORN FART

We all know what a unicorn looks like: It's a horse with a single horn in the middle of its head. It might be flying through the air, or glittering in a magical forest glade, or it might have rainbows streaming out of its tail—there are boundless variations on the precise characteristics of a unicorn, but a child could draw four lines jutting out from the bottom of a round blob, a rectangle pointing upward at an angle from one side of the blob, an oval on top of that rectangle, and a triangle pointing up from that oval, and you could probably guess that it's a picture of a unicorn.

What if motivation is similar? We can all describe it, we generally agree on the characteristics that define it, and you can tell somebody that you felt motivated and he'll know what that means based on what he attaches that label to in his own head.

But I'd say motivation is even less real than a unicorn. Motivation is a unicorn fart. It's the by-product of a bunch of other imaginary things. You get praise, you get your self-esteem up, you reassure yourself, you throw in some affirmations, you judge your internal experience as good, and then you're motivated to do ALL OF THE THINGS.

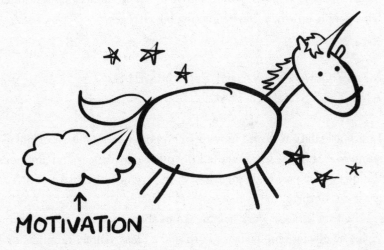

MOTIVATION

That's fine when the feeling's there, but we need to be capable of caring for ourselves even when we don't judge ourselves as motivated. If you feel motivated to make the healthy changes that need to happen and you can sustain that, then carry onward. But if you're like me and you get so motivated to do EVERYTHING and you're incredibly productive for a period of time . . . but subsequently don't feel motivated so you don't do anything, then I'd suggest doing away with the idea of motivation completely. You don't need it. It'll become only another barrier, another feeling to chase. You'll end up constantly judging your feelings to check if you feel motivated enough to do what you need to do. Because motivation is the feeling you want, your brain will make you not feel it so you can keep trying to chase it.

Motivation is like every other feeling we've talked about. You can see that IF X THEN Y dependency at work again. IF X (I don't feel motivated) THEN Y (I can't study). It's the same as IF X (I don't feel calm) THEN Y (I can't talk to people). Judging feelings and then reacting to them is what we're moving away from here. You already know where that practice leads.

Let's look at some supports that can actually help you succeed with making change happen. After that we'll explore something that often trips people up when they're making big changes.

MAKE CHANGE VISIBLE, TANGIBLE, AND CONSEQUENTIAL

I once asked Tom Wujec how to help people overcome all of the assumptions, beliefs, fears, and all the other experiences and emotions that get in the way of change, and Tom very quickly answered: "You get it out of them."

In Tom Wujec's work helping teams solve wicked problems, principles he always emphasizes are to make ideas visible, tangible, and consequential. That's why we've done exercises like the Compulsion Journey. That's an exercise you can go back to if you're finding it difficult to make changes in your life. See why it's difficult and see where you can make changes.

Experiment with this approach of making the stuff in your head visible. It'll keep coming up, for example in the next step, on beliefs and desires—when you'll get your beliefs out of your head and onto sticky notes—but go beyond what I suggest. Just keep pulling things out of your head and making them tangible. As Tom explained to me, "The act of externalizing thoughts—putting things into symbols that are understandable—forces a clarifying function."

Make changes clear. Get them out of the fuzziness of your head. Do this with any change. Here's what that might look like for you: Let's say you want to start exercising more. So you want to make that change visible. You need to see it outside of your head. That probably means writing it down somewhere. But don't stop there. Making it visible isn't always enough. The number of people who love making lists of things they want to do is far greater than the number of people who actually do any of the things on those lists.

The next thing you want to do with this idea is to make it tangible. At the very least, that'll mean writing down the change on something that's physical and movable. Maybe you write a note that says "Go to the gym when you wake up!" and you stick it on your alarm clock so that you have to pick up the note to turn off your alarm.

One of my favorite ways to make an idea tangible is to get an object related to that change and place it in my way. So you might do that by getting your gym clothes ready the night before and putting them right by the door. Make it so you have to step over them. Stick a note on them, too.

Making it consequential is about making these visible, tangible expressions lead to action. To help yourself with that, make sure your reminders are specific. "Leave for the gym at 6:30" is a better note than "Go to the gym." Remove the wiggle room. If you struggle with change, you know your brain is going to exploit every ambiguity it can to reason its way out of this.

You can also introduce some added benefits to going to the gym. Coordinate with another friend to meet at the gym at the same time. Then you get the added benefit of supporting your friend. Not going also has consequences then.

Making it consequential is also about the awareness of how the change aligns with your values. This isn't a random change you're trying to force yourself into. If you don't make this change happen, you're missing out on doing what you actually care about in life. Making this change happen is about being you.

KEEP SUCCESS CLOSE TO YOU

You can support yourself with making change all you want, but the changes you pursue still matter. Always keep in mind what we talked about at the very beginning of the book around goals and goal setting: Keep goals creative and human. I'm also going to expand on that here and suggest that you keep goals close to you and achievable. Even for changes that will take a long time to realize—recovery from an illness, building a business, getting a university degree, becoming a professional sports player, raising a family—bring success into the daily practice of taking steps toward those long-term goals.

For instance, if you want to be a successful musician but you're not currently a musician, that's a far-off goal. Many things need to happen for you to reach that goal. It's going to involve complex changes in your life while navigating a variety of external factors. We want to turn that into something you can actually do today. What you can do today is practice your musical skills. If you practice, then you are successful. If you challenge yourself to use skills you're struggling to master, then you are successful. If you seek help from a teacher to learn about a new technique you can utilize, then you are successful. Measure success by the actions that lead to the outcome you want. That outcome simply becomes a natural side effect of your actions in the present.

Personally, I like to keep success extremely close to me. For me, success is breathing. If I take a breath mindfully, then I've been very successful. All of the practices throughout this book are built on that foundation of mindfulness. So my success is all about a support that I find very useful for doing what I value. Because success is so close to me, it also means that in each moment I can make my next decision from a position of success. I am successful already, so what's the next step I can take to put that success to use in a way that matters to me? Instead of chasing success, I get to spend it.

It seems that people often want to chase success, but when we're struggling with something like anxiety, we're always chasing other things—calm, relief, reassurance, certainty, a way out, the past, recognition—and that puts us in a position of trying to fill an emotional deficit that has nothing to do with what we actually desire.

While acknowledging that any change is a process and often a very long journey, instead of pursuing the outcome of the change, pursue the immediate steps. You're successful with each step. Celebrate those steps. Continually take successful steps and you'll end up much more quickly in the place you want to be.

DON'T GET FOOLED BY ADDICT MATH

The thing most likely to get in the way of making a change in your life is your own brain. Not feeling motivated isn't so much about not having a feeling. It's about our brains coming up with wonderfully logical reasons to avoid change and fall back on what we've done before. I call this "addict math."

You're practicing it when you're trying to start a meditation practice but as you're walking home from work it begins to rain, and you get upset because you wanted to go to the park to meditate. You prefer to meditate in the park because it feels calmer—it's so Zen! There are too many distractions around your house. But now the park isn't an option. Your favorite meditation bench will be all wet. Although maybe this isn't such a bad thing because it's a Friday night and people are supposed to do fun things on Fridays, right? You've been meaning to meditate all week and you haven't done it yet so what's another day? Meditation is more of a Saturday morning type of thing. Maybe the weather will be nice tomorrow so you can meditate in the park then. And you'll be able to meditate for longer because you won't be as stressed as you are right now after such a long week.

The only problem is that when you get home, you remember you don't have any food in the house. You wanted to pick up groceries at a place near the park after you were done meditating so you could make dinner. Now that you're home, you don't feel like going back outside in the rain to walk to the store. You need to relax after a stressful week! And why isn't somebody taking you out for dinner tonight?

You start flipping through dating apps because you'd really like to meet somebody and start a relationship so you don't have to eat alone anymore. But there's always something wrong with each profile you look at. Nobody ticks all of the boxes on your ideal partner checklist. Dating is so frustrating! You wish you could be in a relationship like the couple in the TV series you've been binge watching. Come to think of it, you really want to know how it ends and you've got only a few episodes left. Until you finish the entire series, it'll keep nagging at you in the back of your head and you won't be able to focus on any of the other things you need to get done. So why not just order some takeout, crack open a bottle of wine, and finish off the series? You were trying to stop eating takeout every night and start cooking healthier meals for yourself, but you do need to eat something. It's true that you decided a couple of months ago that you'd drink only when you were with other people, but you were in a serious relationship then. You didn't count on how tough being single would be. You don't need other people to give you permission to do something you want to do. This'll just be one night of indulgence to relax after a long week. Meditating and cooking can wait until tomorrow.

That's addict math. Your brilliant, debate-winning brain can take the tiniest disruption to your plans and spin it into an equation that sends you right back where you don't want to be.

The skills and concepts we explored in the first section of the book will help you get around your brain's arguments. You can accept the stuff in your head and stick to your values instead of engaging in coping or controlling compulsions as a reaction to feelings you don't like. It's okay to feel stressed. You don't have to put that feeling in charge of your life. You can break that IF X THEN Y pattern—brains love to use it when they're engaging in addict math, like IF X (it's raining) THEN Y (I can't meditate). Meditate somewhere else. Get the groceries anyway. You can be flexible and keep your focus on what's important to you over the long term.

If you notice that you're having experiences where you struggle to do the things you actually want to do, that's where you can use the Compulsion Journey exercise to explore the complete system around those changes. If you're arriving at the end of the workweek so exhausted that you can't seem to stop yourself from crashing into a weekend blur of unhappiness and frustration, what changes can you make earlier in the week, at work or at home? The crash at the end of the week is the symptom, not the problem.

There's also one approach that I've found immensely helpful for overcoming addict math and implementing change in my life:

BE UNREASONABLE

You'll always be able to think of a reason not to get out of bed in the morning. You'll always be able to think of a reason not to speak with that person you really want to meet. You'll always be able to think of a reason why exercising is for other people. You'll always be able to think of a reason why the anxieties you're experiencing this time are different, why they seem more legitimate and real, so you should react to them. You'll always be able to think of a reason why today is different and tomorrow is a much better day to get started on doing healthy things. You'll always be able to think of a reason. You're good at thinking.

If you could rationalize and reason your way into better mental health, you would have done it by now. You've thought about it enough.

There's definitely an aspect to building better mental health that's about accepting uncertainty, acting in a way that's aligned with your values, and not engaging in compulsions simply because that's what you do. It's like practicing a piece of music for a performance. You can come up with reasons not to do the practice. You can always make a convincing argument as to why you don't feel like playing right now, why you aren't ready yet to get feedback from a teacher, why you'd rather not struggle with the challenging parts today and exhaust yourself. You might come up with very logical arguments. That's great. But do you want to perform the piece or not? If you do, then you practice.

Making healthy changes requires some unreasonableness.

If you engage in a debate with fear and uncertainty and the urges swirling inside of you, they'll always win. The immediate payoff of reacting to that fear, eliminating uncertainty, and finding relief will always seem to make more sense than sticking to your values and making a decision that's best for you and those around you over the long term. When faced with that angry monster we talked about, it seems to make sense to give it what it wants so it'll leave you alone.

Be brave and unreasonably healthy. Kiss the monster. Tickle it under its chin. Do what you know will make you happy and healthy over the long term because it's what you do, unreasonably.

CAN I DO THIS ON MY OWN?

Maybe. Maybe not.

Committing unreasonably to health is as much about going when you think you should stop as it is about stopping when you think you should go. A runner who pushes through pain could injure herself so badly she wouldn't be able to run anymore. So get help. In the intro-duction, I mentioned supports like connecting with a psychologist or a peer support worker to help guide you on this journey. Sometimes it's not motivation we need but somebody with awareness of the path ahead gently pushing us to take the next step forward.

Working with an experienced professional for your mental health and fitness will be as useful as working with an experienced profes-sional for your physical health and fitness. Look for somebody who knows what works because he lives it and demonstrates that experience. You probably wouldn't want a fitness trainer who's not in great physical shape—how is he going to help you make the changes necessary to live a healthy lifestyle if he can't overcome those challenges himself? The same is true with mental health.

Many people before you have walked the path you're taking. Talk to them. Learn from them. They're not going to know everything that'll happen, but they'll know where many of the hazards are on your path. There's no benefit to stepping in quicksand because you didn't want to get help when any number of mental health adventurers could have told you, "Oh, yeah, don't go that way, you'll get stuck in quicksand." They can help you find a healthy path that you can stay on even when your brain is screaming at you to fall back into your old compulsions.

I wouldn't be where I am now if I hadn't chosen to stop listening to my own brain and start listening to other brains. You can try to do this on your own through trial and error, but if your approach to challenges in the past has led only to more mental health challenges, then it's possible you'll approach this challenge in the same way. Re-member: normal got you here. If you want to get out of the place you're in right now, you're not going to use the brain that knows only how to be in that place.

This might all seem a bit counterintuitive. You need to practice breaking the motivation addiction. The next exercise will help with developing the skills to do just that.

EXERCISE: Practice Not Feeling Right

When learning how to do things you don't feel like doing, as with any exercise, start small. Don't try forcing yourself to make some massive change before you've learned how to make small changes—your head will explode. Instead, bring your awareness to the countless times throughout each day when you put uncomfortable feelings in charge of your life: When you avoid stepping out your door because you hear somebody outside and you don't want to have an awkward conversation with her. When you're in the middle of studying but pull out your phone to check your dating app for messages. When you drop something on the floor and don't pick it up because you can always do it later, and because it's somebody else's job to take care of that anyway. Those are opportunities to experience uncomfortable feelings; accept that they're there, but don't let them control your actions.

I'll list some examples of how to do this exercise, but adapt them to what makes sense in your life. What feelings are you training your brain to avoid? When you encounter that resistance, push into it.

- **Wash your laundry before you absolutely must do it.** Yes, you could leave it until later in the week. There are probably other things you'd much rather do today. You have a clean(ish) pair of underwear somewhere that'll get you through tomorrow. But this is just another way we wait for pressure to build up. We train our brains to act only when the pressure is unbearable. Show your brain that misery does not have to be a prerequisite for action. Do your damn laundry.
- **Respond to messages when you don't feel like responding.** How often have you put off writing an e-mail or a message

because you didn't feel like you were in the right mood or prepared enough to respond? Show your brain that you can write as yourself while you feel anything. Consider your values and write aligned with them. Incorporate this with the checking challenge we covered earlier—send messages when you don't feel like it, without rereading them.

- **Try (not) saying something.** If you notice that you dislike silences and you often speak up to fill them, or you often judge what people are saying as incorrect or critical of you and you feel the need to speak up and correct them, try not saying something next time. Are you creating something with your comments or are you trying to relieve a feeling you don't like? Are you trying to control people to cover up your own insecurities?

  But if you're somebody who often doesn't speak up because you feel uncomfortable talking or because you judge yourself, and you notice that you later regret not standing up for yourself in difficult situations, then practice speaking up. Your silence will create only more suffering.

- **Eat a food you hate.** This is an opportunity to explore why you dislike something. Pick a food that might be useful for you to eat regularly. Try eating it mindfully. Be present to all of the experiences you have as you prepare the food and then eat it. Can you appreciate the food and all of the work that went into getting it to you? Can you like the taste? Where does the dislike come from? Can this food become part of your life?

- **Initiate conversations.** You might see a person you know but you're worried you've forgotten his name, or you're not sure if he's noticed you yet or if he even wants to speak with you, so you hold back and pretend that you haven't noticed him. Don't wait for him to make eye contact with you or to make the first move. You can interact with people. Those feelings and uncertainties can be there. It doesn't matter if you're an introvert or an extrovert. Engaging with people is like building a house—it's a skill. Introverts can be skilled at talking, too.

We stumble over these tiny patches of feelings we don't like as we interact with the world swirling around and through us. Find those moments, notice your attempts to cope and check and control, and go against them in a way that'll be healthy for you and those around you. Add these exercises to your Hierarchy so that you can practice in a structured way. You might decide that for a week you're going to practice initiating conversations with people you sit next to on the bus to work. They don't have to be "good" conversations and people may not want to talk to you. That's totally fine. Like we talked about with success, keep the goal close to you. If you tried to initiate a conversation and that's what you were practicing that week, you were successful. Keep practicing. You'll sweat, you'll push yourself, you'll fail, you'll try again, and it'll get easier.

MAKE SUCCESS POSSIBLE NOW

Throw out unhelpful beliefs and desires

In order to overcome my fear of having a panic attack on an
airplane so I could fly to Cabo San Lucas, I had to change what
I wanted. In the past all I wanted was to not experience anxiety
or panic during a flight. Now my goal was to make it to Cabo
dead or alive.

Cabo was awesome.

—ANTHONY

My long-running dedication to paranoia started when I was quite
young. One of my earliest paranoid memories is of hiding presents
under my bed at Christmastime—not the presents I was giving, but
the presents other people gave me. I did this from when I was a little
kid well into adulthood. I hid the presents there because I knew thieves
were watching our house, and when my family and I went off to visit
our relatives, they would break in and take everything. I hid some of
the presents under the corner of my bed where I thought the thieves
would be least likely to look, and I hid the most valuable stuff under
either the duvet or my pillows because, let's be honest, smart thieves
will look under the bed, but will they look under my pillows?

I would spend the day thinking about the presents, and on the way home I would imagine how we'd pull into the driveway and the thieves would still be there and then I'd have to fight them.

We've already explored how that paranoid streak continued and expanded as my mental illness struggles worsened—I thought people were trying to poison me, trying to steal everything I owned, always spying on me. I was always in danger from something.

The reason I'm mentioning paranoia is because it helped me unravel the much bigger system at work beneath my compulsions. I knew I had to cut out compulsions and I recognized that I was engaging in them as a reaction to fears about getting killed, losing resources, and being alone. So I cut out the compulsions one by one. But I still felt this intense pressure to do them. I still believed I was being watched. I still believed my fears would come true and that all of my fears were terrible things I couldn't experience.

I had reasons for everything going on in my head. Even when I was working with my therapists, I never mentioned paranoia as something that bothered me. I never noticed it because I was always drowning in it. But one day, as I was walking into my living room, I felt the urge to walk differently because I was sure I was being watched through the large window that ran the length of the room, and for the first time I really noticed those thoughts. Why did I believe I was being watched?

As I peeled the compulsions away, I found they were only a component of a system for interacting with the world that kept pushing me toward the compulsions and reinforcing unhelpful beliefs. We looked at this system earlier as a linear system, but now let's look at it as a loop with a new component added in at the center: your beliefs.

Your beliefs are at the core. There's constant feedback between each node in this system and your beliefs.

Throughout this book, you've been learning skills to make changes in this system and dismantle it. Each time you make a change, it's an opportunity to rewrite beliefs. When you practice mindfulness and sit with an experience without trying to control it, you're also helping yourself change your beliefs about whether you can have that expe-

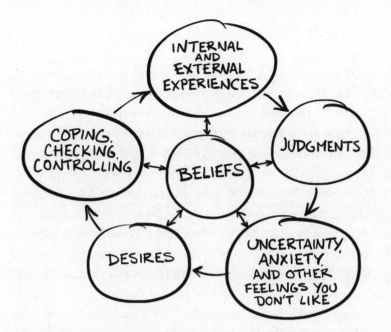

rience. Often, those beliefs are what I call unhelpful beliefs. The belief that I was always being watched is an example. The more changes you can make in this system, the easier and more sustainable your healthy changes will become. If you cut out the compulsions but you don't also throw out the desires, judgments, and beliefs that led to them, you'll constantly find yourself being pushed back into behaviors that cause the same old problems in your life.

For instance, if somebody constantly tries to manipulate others into giving her positive feedback by posting questions on social media about her appearance, and she cuts out that controlling compulsion but doesn't get rid of her desire for positive feedback or her belief that her self-worth depends on what others say, she'll only go hunting for a new compulsion to fulfill that desire and align her experience with her beliefs. It's a recipe for chronic disaster.

BREAK OUT OF BAD FLOW

Spiraling around this system is the mirror opposite of being in a state of flow. I call it bad flow. Flow is a concept developed by psychologist Mihaly Csikszentmihalyi to describe an optimal state of well-being where people are completely immersed in tasks they enjoy and the level of challenge meets their level of skill. When we struggle with mental health, we get locked into bad flow: a nonoptimal state of being where we're completely immersed in tasks that seem to get more and more challenging, taking us further and further away from what matters to us. Everything becomes a crisis when you're in bad flow. Even when there aren't any crises outside of you, they're happening inside of you.

Cutting out compulsions and doing things you value is a helpful step toward getting into that optimal state of flow in your life. It's also important to tackle beliefs, judgments, and desires. Until I dealt with those other components of how I interacted with the world, I was constantly getting pushed into relapse. I felt this never-ending, anxious pressure to get lost again in that bad flow. Bad flow was easy. It's what I'd practiced my entire life. It made me miserable but I was good at it. I struggled to get up and over the Unhappiness Curve, so I kept dropping back on what I'd done before.

In the next chapter, we'll look at judgments and practicing non-judgment. In this chapter we'll look at how you can make changes with beliefs and desires so that you can break out of bad flow.

BELIEFS

It's much easier to throw out unhelpful beliefs than it is to throw out intrusive thoughts, feelings, or urges. That's because you can change your beliefs. Once a thought pops into your head, it has already happened. If you're already experiencing it, the only way not to have that experience would be to travel back in time and not feel it in the first place. If you're not a time traveler, it'll be much easier to change your beliefs about those experiences.

If you believe that dying is a terrible thing to be afraid of, you'll constantly judge the danger and possibility of death around you, you'll want to get rid of the feelings caused by those judgments, and then you'll spend all day compulsively trying to cope with, check on, and control your fear of death, worrying about loved ones dying, spending hours researching cancer symptoms online, ingesting an ever-evolving regimen of supplements and detoxes to ward off the specter of old age, and obsessing over the right items to put on your bucket list.

Or if you believe you should be a good person and thinking bad thoughts makes you a bad person, that'll lead to constantly judging the stuff in your head, trying to correct thoughts, looking for ways to distract yourself from experiences, chasing after the "right" kind of meditation to erase the stuff in your head, trying to avoid situations in life that trigger the thoughts you dislike, progressively shrinking your life.

Or if you believe your value comes from being liked by others, and to be liked you need to have certain material things and accomplish certain milestones, you'll always be chasing things you don't have, judging yourself, judging how people treat you, and basing your self-worth on those judgments. Ideas about attractiveness, status, and value are constantly changing, so you'll be stuck in a never-ending battle to control what others think about you.

Beliefs are choices. Those choices have natural consequences. If you insist on holding on to beliefs that lead to damaging your health, that's a natural consequence of those beliefs. If we choose to hold on to the beliefs that lead to us stumbling back into compulsions, then we're choosing to experience the consequences of those compulsions. Critically reflect on the beliefs you hold. Work backward from your actions to uncover them.

If your beliefs aren't working for you, get new ones. It's your brain, after all.

At every node in that system we looked at—experiences, judgments, the feelings you don't like, desires, and compulsions—you have an opportunity to rewrite your beliefs when you don't move on to the next node in the system. You can experience the desire to spend all night ruminating about an argument you had with your mother, but instead of engaging in that compulsion, you can let that urge be there in your head while you go and work in the community garden down the street. Your actions show your brain that it doesn't need to do something with that urge to ruminate. You don't need to spend those precious moments of your life trying to prove to yourself you were right.

By cutting out compulsions and doing what we value, we start to notice unhelpful beliefs pushing us off course and getting in the way. We're pulling back all the layers of assumptions and judgments that have covered up those beliefs for so many years. We accepted them as truth. It might never have occurred to us that they even were beliefs or anything changeable. We existed in them like fish exist in water.

A set of beliefs you'll probably find useful to change are those about trust, particularly in yourself. Making the changes we've explored and doing more of what you want in life is much easier if you trust yourself.

SHOW YOUR BRAIN THAT YOU TRUST YOURSELF

Do you trust yourself to do things well the first time? Do you trust yourself to act like yourself in any situation? Do you trust yourself not to forget? Not to screw up? Not to embarrass yourself? Not to choose the wrong partner, or the wrong job, or the wrong option on the menu? Do you trust yourself?

It's through our actions that we can show our brains we trust ourselves. Your brain won't learn this by telling it that you're trustworthy. You need to show your brain that you trust yourself. That will change the beliefs you hold about trusting yourself.

I certainly thought I trusted myself, but my actions said something completely different. Every time I went back to check, every time I went digging for reassurance online or from people around me, every time I avoided responsibility or avoided social situations or spent hours ruminating on what to write in an e-mail, and in so many other little actions every day, I was telling my brain: "Don't trust this guy. Worry about what he's done. Don't trust him to handle any problems."

Do your actions show you that you trust yourself? Or do you treat yourself like an incompetent employee you need to micromanage and keep away from important tasks?

In the same way that it's difficult to accept uncertainties that trigger intense amounts of anxiety if you don't first learn how to accept less intense uncertainties, so, too, will you struggle to trust yourself to handle major life decisions and events if you don't learn to trust yourself with the tiny everyday decisions that make up your life.

After years of teaching your brain not to trust yourself, it's time to make trust a practice.

WHAT'S YOUR TRUST SCORE?

Imagine you have a tiny little bank in your brain nestled away in the striatum. Every time you trust yourself, the teeny bankers in this tiny bank keep track of that. They track it with a trust score. It's like your credit score. Every time you accept uncertainty and do something you value, that adds points to your trust score. Every time you feel gratitude and appreciation toward yourself for taking care of yourself, you add a few more points.

Whenever you engage in checking compulsions because of an uncertainty about the past, you knock a few points off. When you engage in controlling compulsions because of your fears about the future, you take more points off. You're telling the bankers: don't trust this person.

When you encounter a big uncertainty that really matters to

you—a decision that you believe will impact your life significantly—you go to the banker in your head to borrow the trust you need to make that leap of faith in yourself. But if you've got a negative trust score, that banker isn't going to lend you the trust to make that leap. And you'll end up falling back on what you've done before.

If we spend all day practicing not trusting ourselves, it's not at all surprising that we don't trust ourselves when we need to the most.

And when I'm talking about trust, I want to emphasize that I don't mean reassuring yourself that your worries won't come true—in other words, trusting that bad things won't happen. That might be what you desire, but that's not what I mean by trust. I mean trusting yourself to handle whatever disasters or successes may come in the future.

DESIRES FOR DISASTERS

It's easy to become overwhelmed by desires. They can swallow up our days and take over our lives. If you desire being rich, but you're not rich, you'll need to spend a lot of time and energy becoming rich. If you're afraid that somebody is threatening your chances of becoming rich or staying rich, that fear can spark many compulsions to control that uncertainty. Those compulsions can lead to your losing everything you've spent so much time chasing. Ask Macbeth about that one.

On a less Shakespearean scale, you can see desires at work behind any compulsion that fuels poor mental health. Maybe you want to be certain that you didn't do something terrible, or you want to feel safe, or you want to know that the person you love loves you, or you want to quiet the shouting in your head, or you want to clear your conscience, or you want people to respect you, or you want acceptance, or you want another doughnut, another drink, another hit, another touch, or you want to feel happy, or you want to prevent people from hurting you, or you want to avoid triggering situations, or you want to get off, or you want to stop panic attacks, or you want to be praised, or you want people to like you, or you want to avoid going broke, getting fired, being hated, or being alone, or maybe you just want to get rid of that constant feeling of anxiety that's always humming through your body every waking minute.

Many of our desires are about wanting not to feel things. People who experience panic attacks may identify a particular situation that brings on an attack, like traveling on an airplane or giving a speech, but research shows that for many of those people, it's not the situation they're actually scared of but the experience of having the panic attack. That desire to avoid the experience leads to the person checking and controlling to make sure it's not happening, which increases his chances of judging something internal or external as a sign that it is happening, which scares him and leads to more attempts to check and control, which leads to it actually happening.

If you want to get rid of anxiety more than anything else in the world, your brain will give you all sorts of things to feel anxious about so you can try to get rid of that feeling and get what you want more than anything else in the world. Your brain is trying to help you. It's giving you the opportunity to get what you want. So be aware of what you desire. If you want nothing more in life than to stop being sad, you will feel sad so you can constantly engage in compulsions to get rid of that feeling. Those compulsions will only lead to you having that experience more, at increasing levels of intensity and complexity. If getting rid of sadness is great, then getting rid of extreme sadness must be even better, right?

SO HOW DO YOU CHANGE A DESIRE?

Well, you don't. It's already there. How could you change it? It'll be more useful to explore how you can handle it, how you can make a mindful decision about what your next step will be. The urge can be there as you take a step toward what actually matters to you.

As your mindfulness practice develops, you can become more aware of desires rising up inside of you. They can feel very enjoyable to entertain and chase after. You might want to send a mean e-mail to a coworker, or maybe quit your job and run off to Thailand in search of yourself, or maybe have one more drink because you deserve it. These are all desires you can have. Like any thought your brain can throw at you, a desire is separate from you. You experience these like any other thoughts or emotions or physical sensations. You can have these experiences and make a decision aligned with your values.

You don't have to change a desire. There are no right or wrong desires. You can experience any desire in the same way that you can walk past a tree on the street, and that doesn't mean anything about you or that you need to do something about that tree. What matters are your actions.

As you change your actions and align them with your values instead of reacting to whatever desire pops up, you'll start to rewrite the beliefs in your brain about what you need to do when you experience a desire. Your brain will start to learn that you don't have to react to every urge.

The Annoying Kids in a Car exercise that we went over in step 12 to help with developing cognitive defusion skills is a useful exercise to practice with desires. Toddlers want everything! Sometimes we do need to listen to what they want. But if we're driving them around to chase after every single one of their whims, we'll never get to travel in a direction that matters to us. You can hear the desires they're shouting from the backseat of the car and you can be empowered to make a decision about where you'll drive. Remember: you control the steering wheel, the brakes, and the gas pedal.

Sometimes, however, we're not clear on exactly what our desires are or how they connect to beliefs. You might struggle even to articulate what your beliefs are. So the next exercise is to help get that stuff out of your head and give you some different perspectives on it.

EXERCISE: Make Your Beliefs Visible

Back when we were talking about how to actually make change happen, I mentioned the importance of that principle I learned from Tom Wujec to always make ideas visible, tangible, and consequential. We'll be putting that to use here again. We're generally much more capable of understanding complex challenges when we externalize our thinking. You can see this in action any time you write down a math equation on paper to help you solve it. The equation doesn't change but your ability to solve it does.

Your beliefs are a dynamic component of the unsolvable equations of life. It's entirely possible that you've never articulated them before. This is an opportunity to get them out in the open:

1. Grab sticky notes or small pieces of paper and something to write with.

2. Write down what you believe. Write only one belief per sticky note. You need to be able to move them around afterward.

3. Get as specific as you can but also look for big, underlying beliefs. So you might list some specific beliefs, such as "I believe my husband loves me when he responds to my messages immediately" and "Getting compliments at work means that I'm valued," as well as some broader beliefs, such as "I need to feel liked." Get them all out there.

4. Now it gets interesting. I'm not going to tell you anything specific to do with them. You need to get creative here. Below,

I'll share some ideas for what you can do with those beliefs once they're out of your head. The purpose here is to help you shift perspective, see which beliefs are helpful and which ones aren't, and begin to recognize that these are changeable, movable ideas. Here are some ideas to explore:

- Try sorting the beliefs. You could move the most problematic ones to the top and the most helpful ones to the bottom.
- Cluster together related beliefs. What do you learn from that?
- Which beliefs are most relevant to your values and which ones seem least relevant?
- Sort the beliefs by which ones are opinions and which ones are facts.
- Which beliefs involve things that are under your control and which involve things not under your control? Cluster them together. How much time do you spend on things not under your control?
- Connect these beliefs to your Inventory. Which beliefs use up the most time and energy?
- Using the Ideal Inventory as a guide, have you missed any beliefs that you might need to hold on to if you want to do the things you have included on it?
- Sort the beliefs by pain—those causing the most pain at the top and those causing the least pain at the bottom.
- Try sorting them on different two-by-two matrices to give yourself four quadrants of beliefs. For example, you could sort by relationships and compulsions. That would show you things like which beliefs are high in relationship significance and high in compulsions, which ones are high in relationship significance and low in compulsions, which are low in relationship significance and high in compulsions, and which are low in both. Or, as in the following illustration, your beliefs can be sorted by beliefs about the past or future, and by which ones are helpful or unhelpful:

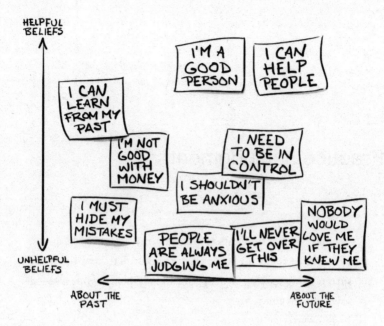

As you go through this exercise, question your assumptions about your beliefs. Be curious instead of judgmental. If you're struggling with your mental health, it's very likely that you're operating with some beliefs that aren't helping you. Get them out of your head and play with them.

Practice nonjudgment

> No matter what thoughts or emotions my brain throws at me,
> I recognize them for what they are, and let them be there,
> surrendering to what is, dropping all judgments, while moving
> toward my values.
>
> —SCOTT

I thought of myself as somebody who was very skilled at judging. I was a quick, accurate judge of character. I could tell what type of person you were after seeing your picture or reading a few sentences you'd written. I knew everything about everybody I saw on the street. I could spot what was going wrong at work before anybody else was aware of it. I knew when a relationship was over before my partner felt it.

That was all part of the problem.

Judgments are a key component of practicing poor mental health. Judgment is the spark that detonates all of the feelings that push us into coping, checking, and controlling. Life will throw enough challenges at you without you creating more for yourself with your judgments.

To understand how to practice nonjudgment, it can help to explore why judgments happen at all. Even if you're the most prolific judger, you already make choices about what you judge, and those choices are wrapped up in your beliefs.

WHY DON'T YOU SPEND ALL DAY JUDGING UGLY PAINT?

Out of the window beside my desk I can see a basswood tree across the street. It's one of the tallest trees on the street. It has branches full of green leaves jutting out from the trunk all the way up. There are thousands of leaves on the tree.

Of those thousands of leaves, some are not perfect. In fact, some are downright ugly. And some are just bad leaves—they're shriveled, they've got holes, they've turned yellow and stopped all of that wonderful photosynthesizing they were doing for the tree.

If you were walking past that tree, why wouldn't you get upset about those leaves? Why wouldn't you spend your day climbing through the tree, fixing the bad leaves, getting angrier and angrier about them? Why don't you do that with every tree you walk past?

If you did put time into judging the leaves and controlling them, it would be just like judging the clouds in the sky, like we discussed back in step 12. There are so many things we're surrounded by that we don't give up time and energy to judge every day. You could wake up every morning and immediately begin to judge the paint on the wall in your bedroom. Many people wake up in the morning and immediately begin to ruminate and obsess about all of the things they're worried about. They obsess about what they're obsessing about. They get upset about the feelings of anxiety that swamp them as soon as they open their eyes. But not many people wake up judging the paint in their room. Why don't you judge the paint? Throughout your day, you probably see many painted walls and some of them are surely ugly shades of peeling, faded, outdated colors. So why don't you devote all of your time and energy to fixing all of that ugly paint?

The more you practice mindfulness and meditation, the more you'll find space between you and your internal experiences. It's in that space that you can start to make choices about what you'll do with an experience. You can choose whether to judge it. Practicing nonjudgment doesn't mean you agree with the experience. It doesn't mean you negate the experience. The thought, feeling, or physical sensation is there, like a leaf on a tree, paint on a wall, or a cloud in the sky. It's part of your experience. As you practice cognitive defusion with these experiences and put some space between you and them, in the gap you'll find beliefs underneath your judgments—beliefs about what should and shouldn't happen, how things should or shouldn't be. Are those beliefs useful to you?

Personally, one of the most interesting areas within which to explore my judgments and to practice nonjudgment was with my internal experiences, like emotions and physical sensations.

Our bodies are amazing. Sometimes they even work relatively well. There's so much going on in them. At this moment, you could judge any number of physical or emotional experiences you're having. There'll be many great experiences and a couple of nasty ones all happening simultaneously. Those experiences are like leaves. You can be aware of them and choose what you want to do with them. But all of those experiences are filtered through your brain. Do you believe what your brain tells you?

I've learned not to believe mine—believing the stuff that comes out of my brain is a one-way ticket to Crazy Town. The challenge, however, is that our perceptions of physical experiences can be very useful to living our lives. If a knife gets too close to your finger and you feel some pain, you can recognize that and pull your finger away so you don't slice it off. In that situation, it's useful to recognize that pain and take action. If you don't, you'll lose a finger. But if you're struggling with emotions and thoughts and other mental experiences you don't like, there's a very good chance you'll also be struggling to handle physical experiences. Through practice, your brain can judge all physical sensations as indicators of imminent danger, triggering anxiety and a flight-or-flight response, whether or not it's actually useful to you. Let's look at some examples:

MISOPHONIA, VOMIT, AND PEEING MY PANTS

One of the ways my mental health issues manifested in physical sensations came in the form of what's known as misophonia. Basically, I couldn't tolerate particular sounds. The sounds were physically uncomfortable and over several years they progressively became unbearable.

I couldn't stand to be around the sound of chewing. To this day, even though I can now be around people chewing loudly and I don't have problems with any sounds, when I recall memories of being around people chewing loudly in the past, my arms tingle and I can feel that panicked urge to get away, just like I would back then. It's seared into my nervous system.

The physical discomfort I experienced from the sounds I hated was an experience I didn't want to have. I didn't believe I could do anything I wanted to do while I experienced that discomfort, so I went out of my way to avoid the sounds I hated. Once the sound was gone, the uncomfortable feeling in my body would dissipate, and I would get on with whatever I was doing. But the more I engaged in those compulsions to avoid and control sounds, the less tolerance I had for them.

This wasn't the only physical experience that challenged me. I hated vomit and all of the physical experiences connected with it. Until I was in my thirties, I did everything humanly possible to avoid eating eggs or oatmeal. That was mostly about the texture, although even the smell of eggs could make me feel nauseated and like I was about to vomit. I hated eggs more than anything else on the planet. Similar to the sounds I avoided, it wasn't an intellectual decision to dislike eggs. My body hated eggs.

I struggled with my perceptions of what was happening in my

body. The slightest bit of nausea could trigger worries about vomiting. An odd pain in my side would set me off Googling about cancer or HIV. Before doing anything I thought of as important, like a big presentation at school, I would go to the bathroom multiple times. I truly felt like I did need to pee, badly, and if I didn't go, I was convinced I'd have an accident in front of everybody while I was presenting.

When things were at their worst, I wanted to be a rock alone in a desert, everything barren for miles around so there was no chance of experiencing anything inside or outside of me that I didn't control.

The physical sensations I experienced in all of those examples were real experiences. They were as real as experiencing anxiety. Anxiety is a real experience. An image popping into my head of me stabbing somebody is also a real experience. Seeing a leaf on a tree is a real experience. I can choose what I do with these experiences. I can judge them or not. So what did I do with the sounds and the vomit and peeing?

I practiced experiencing them on purpose. I sought out the sounds I hated and experienced the physical reactions to them, recognizing that I had flexibility in what I did with those experiences and what meaning I attached to them.

I ate eggs every day for a month. That was about showing my brain it was wrong about eggs and vomit. I practiced liking the eggs and liking the idea of becoming nauseated and vomiting. If I vomit, that's okay! I can vomit everywhere! I would like nothing more in the morning than to get on a streetcar and vomit on everybody!

You can see that ACT structure there again and the second trick, of accepting the consequences.

I stopped going to the bathroom before important events when I felt like I needed to go. I started eating again before those events to fuel being myself. I would agree with my brain that I was in desperate need of a toilet and I was going to soil myself. In fact, I would tell myself I probably already had, and I wasn't going to check, I was going to walk straight into that presentation with a big wet stain on my pants and introduce myself, smiling to everybody.

TRY CURIOSITY INSTEAD OF JUDGMENT

In his book *You Are Here*, Thich Nhat Hanh suggests taking a piece of paper, writing on it "Are you sure of your perceptions?" and then sticking that on a wall. Grab a sticky note, write it down, and keep it where you can see it because that monster up in your head will try anything to get you to feed it compulsions again, including giving you the real physical experiences that terrify you the most.

If you struggle with physical experiences when you're about to do something stressful or new—maybe when you're about to go on a date or volunteer to do something at work you've never done before—try to welcome them with curiosity. Can you let that sensation or that discomfort be there? What does it feel like? Where do you feel it? What anxieties is it triggering? Try going through the Five Whys exercise we covered earlier. Is your body responding to a fear? What is your body trying to help you prevent by offering you this warning, even if turns out to be a false alarm? What are those annoying kids in the backseat crying about? Are they threatening you with pee on your new car's upholstery because they want to avoid the place you're taking them?

Exploring physical sensations with curiosity is a practice you can then extend to any experience, like anxiety or the urge to engage in a behavior you want to cut out. You can be curious about those experiences instead of judging them and triggering the feelings that make compulsions seem necessary.

WILL PRACTICING NONJUDGMENT MAKE ME A BAD PERSON?

Nonjudgment is the topic about which I receive the most passive-aggressively angry messages. I think it's very misunderstood. Practicing nonjudgment isn't about practicing it to the exclusion of judgment. It's about developing the capacity to have a choice. It's about recognizing that running up to every person you see and wrapping them up in labels before hitting them on the head with all of your baggage isn't the best approach in every situation. It's about giving you freedom, the freedom to create and build what you want to see in your life and your community.

Do you currently have the ability *not* to judge something? Can you meet somebody without judging her? Can you hear a song and hear only the music, not your judgments about that type of music or what it might mean about you to listen to it? Can you feel a physical sensation in your body without judging it as something that shouldn't be there? Can you prevent a bad day from derailing your life? Can you fail? Can you appreciate yourself without grasping after valuables and judging your worth based on them? Can you look in the mirror without seeing a problem to fix?

When you judge a voice in your head as an experience you shouldn't have, when you judge a pain inside of you as wrong, when you judge an urge as something that needs relieving, when you judge an error at work as career ending, when you judge an intrusive thought as blasphemous, when you judge yourself as disgusting, when you judge anxiety as something you shouldn't feel, when you judge your partner as abandoning you because you can see they're online but they're not messaging you—these all have predictable outcomes: more struggling and suffering.

Judgment is the first compulsion. The feelings you don't like that come after your judgments are totally natural and inevitable. If you want to put an end to those inevitabilities, learn how to practice nonjudgment. Give yourself the choice. There's incredible freedom when a thought is a thought, a text message is a text message, your gut is your gut, a car is a car, and you can make decisions based on your values while experiencing whatever you're experiencing.

Practicing nonjudgment doesn't mean we give up on what we value for ourselves or our communities. Practicing nonjudgment is part of the transformation from a fear-fueled life to a values-fueled life. Practicing nonjudgment means you're no longer confined by the judgment machinery in your head. It means you can do the things you value, not because you're forced to or because it would be wrong not to, but because it's in those actions where you find long-term benefit for yourself and your community.

Give nonjudgment a chance. After years of becoming an expert judger, it'll be tough at first. But you'll soon find you have so many other uses for that brain power you're currently pumping into judging everything. Next up are some exercises to help you get started with understanding how your brain judges and how you can practice nonjudgment.

EXERCISE: Nonjudgment Practice

If you were performing a complex weight-lifting maneuver in the gym, like a clean and jerk, you'd break it down into its component movements to help you understand how to do the exercise effectively. We're going to do the same for nonjudgment, which is a component of mindfulness and, in a broader sense, a component of learning how to cut out compulsions and do things you value.

There are two things in particular to pay attention to when you're practicing nonjudgment during the activities coming up:

1. Can you prevent the judgment that triggers the feelings you don't like? It'll be tough at first, but try to develop an understanding of how that judgment happens.

2. When you do judge things, can you choose to do something you value instead of engaging in a compulsion and giving up control of your life to that judgment?

Here are the activities:

1. The nonjudgment walk.

Go to a busy place where you can walk around. It might be a mall at peak shopping hours, or a busy city neighborhood at rush hour. Practice mindful walking. Get pushed. Get cut off by cars. Hear people shout. Hear babies cry. See things you hate. See things you love. Discover things you crave. Notice whatever pops into your head. Can you see people without judging them? Can you see their actions as actions, without attaching any extra labels to them? When you notice judgments exploding in your head, can you bring your awareness back to the present moment? Can you enjoy being you?

2. The wrong opinions.

Watch a news network that features shows and pundits you disagree with vehemently. You can also do this with a TV show you hate, or one that you often avoid because you think it's stupid or crass. Sit in front of those shows. Notice how judgments emerge in your head. Can you hear people say things that are wrong, accept that they're wrong, but not let their words take control over your mood? Can you be you while hearing and seeing things that are wrong? Instead of getting angry about fixing wrong opinions, can you get excited about pouring yourself into building a community that's healthy for you and those around you?

3. The distracted worker.

Do your work in a busy, noisy place. I especially like to do this exercise in chaotic mall food courts or on public transit. I'll write something that I know I'll be sending to somebody or publishing online. That makes my brain worry about making a mistake because I'm not writing in the "right" type of place.

Don't try to block out the noise with headphones. Notice how you judge the environment and your ability to work in it. Notice how you judge people who annoy you. Can you identify what you value in getting that work done? Can you align your actions with your values, recognizing that controlling your environment and those around you is not something you're able to do? Can you bring your awareness back to your work when your thoughts start chasing after judgments about things happening in your environment?

EVERYTHING IN YOUR HEAD IS WEATHER

Make happiness a practice

When I've felt things I want to brush off and deny as real, they always come back to haunt me and make me unhappy. To handle them, the first step I take is giving those feelings some space to exist. Then I try to express them in a real way, like writing them down, talking about them with someone I trust, or even taking a photo that helps me remember them. Even if taking a photo doesn't say exactly what I'm feeling in words, it becomes a mental bookmark for me to reference bad feelings—and make something in the process that connects with what I'm passionate about.

—MATT

As you learn to practice nonjudgment and you're not constantly judging yourself and the world around you, you'll notice that you experience less of the feelings you don't like: fear, anxiety, anger, frustration, envy, disappointment, and so on. But the absence of fear is not the presence of happiness. Like we've discussed, pursuing escape from those feelings as a goal will lead only to more of them. Happiness is its own distinct practice.

Earlier, when we talked about switching the fuel for your life from fear to values, I shared that story about walking out in the morning and panicking because I had nothing to be anxious about. One of the factors that made me so anxious was that I didn't know how to be happy without having fear or anxiety to control and then feel happy about controlling. For my entire life, I believed happiness meant controlling my fears. Fear and anxiety were necessary for my experience of happiness. I thought I could be happy only when I defeated my enemies.

If you believe that happiness comes only after defeating enemies, then you need to keep enemies in your life. Any happiness you find on the other side of defeating an enemy will quickly fade and you'll need to find a new one to battle. If you take that approach with things like anxiety or stress or relationship problems, you'll always be bringing problems back into your life in search of happiness on the other side of them. More happiness will require increased levels of stress and anxiety and heartbreak. If you believe you'll be happy only when you're certain people respect you, you'll require uncertainty about being respected. If you believe you can be happy only when you get rid of intrusive thoughts, you'll require intrusive thoughts, at ever-increasing levels of severity. If you want to eliminate the urge to engage in whatever your addiction might be so that you can finally be happy, or do your work, or have a meaningful relationship, the cravings become even more totalizing because you've made the battle with them a prerequisite to living your life. That's the fear-fueled approach to happiness. With that approach, you commit yourself to constant, never-ending war with the experiences you hate.

End the war.

You don't have to win it. You don't have to prove anything wrong. You don't have to make your fears go away. You don't have to be certain. Leave the uncertainties hanging there.

Walk off the battlefield.

Let the things you hate scream and shout at you. They can hang around and watch you build happiness. Their presence doesn't negate or contradict happiness unless you stop the practice of happiness and go off and fight them, leaving happiness neglected.

Walking off this battlefield is challenging. As much as you might hate fighting and struggling with the enemies inside of you, you might not know of any other way to live. Your identity might have become very dependent on your enemies.

YOU MIGHT HAVE STOCKHOLM SYNDROME

You've been kidnapped. Your kidnapper beats you and keeps you locked in a cage that he's forced you to help him build. He's threatened your family and your friends. He's taken you away from everything you've always dreamed about. He verbally harasses you and emotionally torments you. You don't dare try to venture out of your cage for fear of punishment. You're terrified that he could pop out from behind a corner at any moment. He's imprinted this fear into your gut so intensely that he doesn't even have to lock the tiny, cramped cage to which you've willfully confined your life. You could leave, but what if he comes back? What would he do to you? What if you start doing something you'd always wanted to do and then he shows up? What if it's worse than last time? And, really, it's not so bad being trapped here anyway. You don't have to worry about all sorts of things that bothered you in the past. They're out of your life now. And even though he beats you and ruins your life, he does give you pizza and ice cream. There are far fewer things to worry about when you live in a cage. Besides, the bars of your cage aren't actually trapping you, they're protecting you! There are worse catastrophes out there! You know because you've worried about them. You've imagined them in painstaking, bone-aching detail. Being in this cage is simply who you are. It's for the best. You're not like other people. And you're happy in the cage. . . . Well, maybe *happy* isn't the right word. You're mildly not panicked . . . right now. That's like happiness, right?

One of the biggest challenges I see people encountering on the journey to building better mental health is that they develop Stockholm syndrome with their compulsions. Stockholm syndrome is a term given to describe the experience of identifying with and even defending your kidnappers or abusers. On one hand, you hate the experience of being trapped and anxious and not being able to live your life the way you want to. On the other hand, you really enjoy the brief moments of relief and certainty that come from trying to control your fears and avoid feelings you don't like.

People can complain for years about their struggles with anxiety, absolutely hate the compulsive behaviors that they engage in, feel miserable about the opportunities they let slip by because they listened to the fears their brains threw at them, and still, when offered the chance to change, many, if not most, will turn down the opportunity to escape. The change looks too difficult, too uncertain, and they worry about losing the perceived benefits of their compulsions. They cease to recognize that they're in a prison. They start to believe the bars are actually protecting them, not trapping them. Their hatred for their symptoms is only trumped by their fear of actually escaping them.

Expect this to happen. After years of repeatedly pacing around this prison, your brain will not want to leave it. The kidnapper it knows causes less anxiety than the freedom it doesn't understand.

TRACK FUNCTIONING, NOT FEELINGS

You're going to walk off that battlefield, you're going to step out of that prison, and you're going to start doing the things you've always wanted to do, and it's entirely possible it'll feel terrible.

When you're first making big changes in your life, you'll be riding up and down the Unhappiness Curve over and over again. You're innovating. As you're making the shift from a fear-fueled, reactive life to one that's fueled by your values, you'll struggle. You'll feel things you hate. You'll often feel like you're failing, that things will never get better, that you don't deserve to get better, that it's too challenging, that it's not working. Think all of that and more. Feel it all. Make space for it. With time and practice, you'll be able to welcome those experiences with gratitude and compassion. To start with, simply allowing them to be there without letting them throw you off course is enough. We can practice mindfulness with whatever we're feeling or thinking.

This might sound strange, but the practice of happiness isn't about feeling happy right now. It's about doing the things that help you be happy and healthy over the long term. Happiness is a natural result of doing what you value. In the short term, aligning your actions with your values won't necessarily make you feel happy. When you're accepting uncertainty, anxiety, and other feelings you don't like and aligning your actions with your values instead of reacting with compulsions, you'll often feel terrible. It's stressful. Building great mental health and emotional fitness is messy, like improving physical fitness. You will doubt yourself. You will think you're failing. You will want to quit. You'll feel weak. You'll feel like you're not improving.

Don't leave this journey up to your brain's perception of what you're feeling and how you're progressing. Remember that sticky note: "Are you sure of your perceptions?" Instead of relying on your brain's perceptions of your feelings, track functioning.

Functioning is your ability to do what you want to do in life. Improving mental health is all about functioning—developing the capacity to feel whatever you're feeling while doing what matters to you. Track that capacity to do what matters to you. Are you continuing to cut out compulsions on your Hierarchy? Are you consistently doing the activities on your Awesome Schedule? Are you practicing nonjudgment? Are you accepting whatever uncertainties that monster in your head throws at you? Are you sticking to your values with each step you take?

The practice of being yourself, even when it leads to experiences you don't like, can still be a practice full of happiness. You may discover, however, that you're not as skilled at feeling happiness as you are at feeling things like anxiety and fear. To help you stay outside the cage or off the battlefield, we need to work on developing your capacity to experience feelings you like.

HAPPINESS IS TOUGH

It's tough to feel happy. Hating people is easy. Trying to avoid pain is easy. Trying to control uncertainty is easy. These are all practices that make us miserable and hurt us, but they're easier than feeling happiness and risking its loss. It's easy to say that I'm trapped in a cage right now so I can't do the things I want to do in life. It's easier to react to the fear of an enemy than it is to step off the battlefield into the uncertainty and freedom of creating your life.

In the chapter on coping compulsions, we talked about accepting feelings we don't like, but are you also willing to accept happiness? Or love? Developing your emotional fitness isn't only about learning how to handle feelings you don't like. Accepting feelings like love and happiness will help you do more of what makes you happy. It will help you deepen your relationships. It will help you prevent yourself from dropping back into the familiar comfort of constantly trying to solve the feelings you hate.

Feelings like love and happiness are also experiences we try to control because we're unsure of how to handle them. We stick extra meanings onto them. We become afraid of losing what we've always wanted. We get caught in IF X THEN Y loops. We push people away because we don't want to get hurt or we don't want to hurt them.

Are you skilled at feeling anxious? Do you have great endurance when it comes to hating? Can you spend a day being upset about a comment a stranger made online? Can you spend an entire week being anxious about a project at work, from the moment you wake up each day until you knock yourself out with sleeping pills at night? Can you spend a month hating your ex-boyfriend, constantly obsessing about him, time traveling into the past to argue with him?

These are incredible skills that require impressive endurance. It speaks to the years of practice we invest in feeling anxiety and hatred that we can hold these emotions for such long periods of time.

We can do the same with emotions like happiness, love, or compassion. But they require a similar amount of practice. In the same way that we practice compulsions to give ourselves more of the emotions we don't like, we can practice skills like mindfulness, we can embrace uncertainty, and we can do things we value to experience more of the feelings we do enjoy. One of the ways we can improve our ability to experience happiness is through the practice of gratitude.

YOU CAN EXPRESS GRATITUDE IN ANY MOMENT

What I find most effective is bringing the practice of gratitude into my daily life with the simplest of activities. It's not about adding up the "good" things that happened and feeling grateful for them. It's about feeling grateful for what I'm doing. If I'm making myself a sandwich, I can be grateful for nourishing myself. When I'm sitting and breathing, I can be grateful for my lungs. They do so much work for me and I don't even ask them to do it! I can be grateful for the floor beneath me. It's holding me up! I can be grateful for the ability to read and write. How else could I find the word *chocolate* so quickly on the dessert menu? I can be grateful for all of the people who worked to build the place in which I live. Maybe those people are all dead now but I can experience their hard work. I can feel gratitude toward the people I walk past on the street. It's much more enjoyable to feel gratitude than to feel fear or hatred or disgust or envy. Those people don't need to do anything specific for me. Feeling gratitude toward somebody is an enjoyable experience without requiring a reason to do it.

When I'm getting ready to leave in the morning, I can feed myself, wash myself, brush my teeth, clip my nose hairs, clean my ears, put on clothes, and do whatever else I might do as practices of gratitude and appreciation to myself. I could do all of that out of fear of what I think others will think about me, or maybe out of fear for my health or my career, or I can do them as a way to practice gratitude and appreciation for myself and my body. It all depends on what skills I want to practice and what I want my brain to think about during the day.

If you spend a significant amount of time getting ready in the morning, doing your hair or putting on makeup or coordinating the perfect outfit, that practice can become an opportunity to feel gratitude toward yourself. If you spend that time each morning appreciating your body, you'll discover that this practice has many benefits throughout your life. If you spend that time each morning trying to control your body or appearance in the hopes of manipulating what others think about you, that's a serious amount of time invested in fear and anxiety, which will also have very natural results (which you won't like).

You don't need to find more time in your life to feel gratitude toward yourself. You can take advantage of what you're already doing simply by changing your intentions. Again, this is about making the switch from fear-fueled actions to values-fueled actions:

- Instead of brushing your teeth because you want to avoid bad breath or make sure there isn't a piece of spinach stuck there, try brushing your teeth as appreciation for all of the hard chewing those teeth have done for you.

- Instead of putting on your clothes while obsessing about what you think those clothes will make others think about you, try putting on your clothes as a way of expressing yourself, or keeping yourself warm, or keeping yourself comfortable. It's also an opportunity to feel gratitude to all of the people who worked to make those clothes. It's very likely that somebody on the other side of the world stitched together the clothes you're wearing, in a workplace that you couldn't imagine working in, for an amount of money that you couldn't imagine living on. You are connected to a global network of people who make your life possible.

- Instead of eating to control your body, or punish it, or chase away feelings, try eating to fuel the practice of being you. You're giving energy to each cell in your body. Offer that food in gratitude to all of the organs inside you that work tirelessly day and night to keep you alive. Feel gratitude toward all of the people who worked to bring that food from the fields to your stomach. If you're eating an animal, don't ignore that. It was alive once, like you. You can appreciate what it means to be alive.

There are so many opportunities to practice gratitude in your daily life while doing the things you're already doing. Explore why you do what you do. What do you want your brain to think about? Are you starting off your day with an hour or two of meditation on anxiety or gratitude? That's your practice. Practice whatever skill at which you hope to become adept.

I understand how difficult it can be to even imagine thinking positively about yourself, let alone expressing feelings of gratitude toward yourself or others on a regular basis. The exercise for this step is a very old and popular practice that will help you develop the capacity to feel and express emotions like gratitude, compassion, kindness, and love.

EXERCISE: Loving-Kindness Meditation

I typically take my meditation the same way I take my green tea: with no extra things in it. But I do make some exceptions with my meditation practice (although never with tea), and loving-kindness, or *metta*, meditation is one such exception.

Loving-kindness meditation is a practice that got me into the idea of emotional fitness because I found it so difficult to feel emotions like love and kindness and gratitude, particularly toward myself. It was physically very difficult for me to feel love toward myself. As with any exercise, that difficulty is a helpful sign of something that needs practicing.

I'll include a written guide here that you can read through, but I encourage you to seek out audio guides you can follow, try different styles, work with experienced teachers in person—whatever helps you build up your skills with this practice. This is valuable for building capacity to feel emotions you might not practice nearly as much as you practice emotions you hate. You can't expect your brain to be skilled at feeling love and kindness without deep practice.

1. Grab a seat and get comfortable.

2. Close your eyes and breathe normally. Notice where you're in contact with the floor or the seat beneath you. Be with that awareness for several breaths.

3. Then slowly bring your awareness up your body. Take a couple of breaths at each body part. Say hello to each one. Notice the posture of your body. Bring your awareness up your torso to your chest.

4. Be aware of breathing in. Be aware of breathing out.

5. Spend some time meditating like this, slowing down your thoughts, getting your brain to sit with you as you breathe. Notice whatever you're feeling and welcome that. You might be anxious. You might want to think about problems at work or school or in a relationship. That's all okay. When

your thoughts start to run off again, gently bring your awareness back to your breath. Notice the physical sensations of your body moving with each inhale and each exhale.

6. When you're ready, bring to mind something that makes you feel happy and warm and loving. It might be a person, an animal, a particular event, or a place. Whatever it is for you, picture it in your mind. Experience it. Be aware of the physical experience you have around that thing you love. Breathe into that feeling and let it extend to every part of your body.

7. If you notice your awareness has wandered off to worry about whether you're in the wrong career or if that pain in your gut is cancer, simply return to the thing that gives you that warm, loving feeling and breathe that feeling back into your body.

8. Whatever you brought to mind to give you that loving feeling, express that feeling back toward it in gratitude. Feel that loving-kindness flow from you into it.

9. If you want to express that feeling of loving-kindness in words, go for it. Wish health, and happiness, and freedom. But continue to feel that expression of emotion at a level deeper than words. See it flowing out of you.

10. Repeat steps 8 and 9, and each time bring to mind a different person to express loving-kindness toward. Here's a suggestion on how you might structure this:

- Begin with somebody you care for deeply, somebody you would be happy to see.

- Then move on to an acquaintance you have no particular feelings about. Enjoy feeling loving-kindness
toward somebody who owes you nothing and to whom
you owe nothing.

- Then bring to mind somebody you hate. It could be
somebody who has hurt you or hurt people around you.
Notice the judgments and thoughts that arise around
that person. You don't have to argue with him or prove
him wrong. Feeling loving-kindness toward him does
not change or contradict anything he's done to you or
to anybody else. Can you express love and kindness
toward somebody who has caused pain to you or those
you care about? This isn't supposed to be easy. You're
building and growing. Can you feel compassion for a
person because they're a person?

- Then try feeling loving-kindness toward yourself. This
might be even more difficult than loving somebody who
has hurt you. Can you look past your judgments of
yourself and embrace you for being you?

- To finish, you could bring to mind a group of people,
like your community, some people you know are struggling, or perhaps the entire world. Spread that feeling
of loving-kindness to all of them. Enjoy that connection
with so many people.

- If at any point you feel your loving-kindness batteries
depleting, return to that initial thing that helped you bring
up the feeling.

- Take as much time as you need with this. There's no
need to rush through. Enjoy the practice!

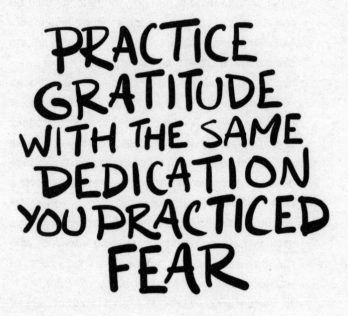

Embrace uncertainty

The main challenge for me in recovery from OCD was trusting that the obsessions and fears weren't true. I only turned the corner toward recovery when I surrendered to the idea that I may never know, and only then did OCD loosen its grip. The only thing that is certain is uncertainty, and that's okay!

—STUART

We're constantly encountering new uncertainties around us, or dragging old ones along with us from the past, or inventing new ones about the future, all on our own. If you hold on to beliefs about uncertainty being a very bad thing or something that needs resolving, then practicing happiness can become very difficult because doing things you value will require you to leave many uncertainties unresolved. Even if you don't engage in compulsions to resolve uncertainties, you'll still constantly experience uncertainty as you grow and change and people in the world around you do the same. That can be a very unpleasant and stressful experience or it can become an experience that helps you thrive. In this step we'll unpack some of the uncertainty baggage you might be carrying around with you and we'll look at how pushing into uncertainty is the path forward to being yourself.

SEEKING OUT UNCERTAINTY

This goes all the way back to that very first exercise we did to practice not checking our phones. I emphasized then the importance of tackling easier uncertainties so you can develop the capacity to handle the ones that actually bother you. Now, with everything you've learned, consider how you can take that simple exercise and turn it into a lifestyle that supports doing what you value.

You don't even have to wait for uncertainties to pop up. You can seek them out. When you get the urge to Google the guy you're about to go out on a date with, can you sit with that uncertainty and then make a decision about whether it's a useful way to invest your time? Can you take on a new task at work that's unfamiliar and admit that you don't know what you're doing? Can you sit in that uncertainty and learn new skills? Can you take on a challenge when you don't know if you'll fail or succeed? Maybe you can't lift that weight, or you won't pass the test, or there won't be anybody there you know, or you will be responsible for things going wrong. . . . Can you accept those uncertainties and still be yourself while you take steps forward? Can you enjoy those steps without chasing any special reward for them?

When you start to take this broad approach to embracing uncertainty, every moment of the day becomes an opportunity to care for your mental health and develop your capacity to handle experiences you avoided in the past. Every time you find an uncertainty to embrace, you free up a little bit more of your time and energy to spend on things that actually matter to you.

SO DO I HAVE TO SPEND THE REST OF MY LIFE DOING THINGS THAT MAKE ME ANXIOUS?

Imagine that a kid named Simon goes to the zoo with his middle school class. Simon really wants to see the chameleons. He's a huge fan of chameleons. He knows everything there is to know about them. They have cells called chromatophores that help them change color, and their eyes can look in two directions at once, and their tongues can be twice the length of their bodies. They are AMAZING. His mom won't let him have one, so he's superexcited to see live chameleons at the zoo today.

But when he gets off the bus with the other students, the big popular school bully slaps him on the back of the head and says, "Hey, new guy, come and check out the rhinos with us."

Simon is new to this school and he doesn't have many friends. He's afraid that if he doesn't go with the popular kids, they'll be mean to him in the future, so he goes along with them to see the rhinos, even though he thinks rhinos are boring. He's worried about having time to see the chameleons. The reptile exhibit is on the other side of the zoo from the rhinos.

The boys throw some rocks at the rhinos and try to scare them but the rhinos don't do anything. One of the boys suggests they go and see the tigers next door. Simon thinks about excusing himself from the group but that only makes him anxious. Would they think he doesn't like them? Would they be mean to him later? How would he even tell the group he was leaving without it being really awkward? What if they think chameleons are lame? He decides to stay. He'll try to be like a chameleon and blend in with the group. He can make the same jokes about the girls. He can say cool things and be cool so people think he's cool.

Simon is very small and he's always afraid that other boys won't think he's tough. When he sees the tigers sleeping in their pen, he says, "I thought they would look scarier. They look like house cats." He thinks that's a very tough thing to say and that people will think he's tough now. But what actually happens is that the bully says, "I dare you to touch one. Just run in, touch it, and run back." And then two of the other boys grab Simon, easily lift him up, and toss him over the fence into the tiger enclosure.

Simon has never been so afraid in his life. A tiger opens its eyes and snarls at him. His heart is racing. He's so panicked that his head feels like it's about to explode. He doesn't know what to do. He doesn't know what's going to happen. But he's heard that reacting to anxiety and uncertainty is a compulsion. He's very anxious right now and incredibly uncertain about whether he'll get mauled by a tiger. So does that mean he needs to touch the tiger? That he should push into this uncertainty? Is it a compulsion to avoid his fear? Isn't he supposed to turn toward difficult emotions?

The tiger eats Simon.

If we look at the big picture of what happened that day, there was a series of compulsions that led to Simon being in that tiger's stomach: reacting to the uncertainty about being liked, trying to control what others thought about him, not being honest, etc. Whether it's a compulsion or not to avoid touching the tiger is irrelevant. By consistently controlling and avoiding uncertainty about what might happen if he went and did what he wanted to do, he very naturally ended up in a situation that created even more uncertainty and fear.

Improving emotional fitness and learning how to handle internal and external experiences are things we do in service of and aligned with our values. We're not doing this for the sake of doing it. We're doing it to live our lives.

PICK YOUR (CREATIVE) BATTLES

You can draw a line from where you are to where you want to be, like a path through uncharted wilderness, and that path will take you through an astounding number of uncertainties. That path will also be surrounded by uncertainties on all sides calling for your attention. Embracing uncertainty is as much about charging headfirst into the uncertainties that obscure the path ahead as it is about walking past the uncertainties that lie off your path. There's nothing wrong with uncertainties. You don't have to solve them simply because they exist. If you step off to chase after them, you'll never get to where you want to be and you'll spend the rest of your life digging in the undergrowth for certainty about things you don't even care about.

In the past, if I read something that I didn't know about in an article, I'd immediately look it up, and then I'd discover something in that article I didn't know about, so I'd dig up a documentary on that and spend two hours watching it out of the corner of my eye while sitting on the sofa, checking my messages on my phone, reading the news, and looking up more things I didn't know about. I was like a raccoon trying to catch the water spraying out of a lawn sprinkler. The flow of uncertainties didn't stop and I didn't stop trying to resolve them.

But when I experience uncertainties like those, I need to reflect on whether reacting to them will help me do something I value or if it's simply my brain trying to chase certainty like a dog that runs after every stick. I liked spending my time chasing after every little thing that interested me. I hated that I never accomplished any of the things that I actually wanted to do.

This isn't about stifling creativity, curiosity, or exploration. This is about being able to choose the uncertainties you do explore. It's about seeing what's useful for creating and building.

If you're about to get in an argument with your partner because you want to correct something she said, ask yourself how resolving that will help you create the relationship you want to have with your partner. If you're about to embark on learning a new skill, ask yourself if that's going to help you do the types of things that help you find meaning in life. If you're about to do an exposure exercise because you want to get over a fear, ask yourself if you're doing this to experience more in life or if you're doing it because you're afraid of fear and want to avoid it.

BUT WHAT IF I'M UNCERTAIN ABOUT THE PAST?

We've mostly been exploring uncertainty in the present, but many of the uncertainties you might be troubled by or trying to resolve will be from the past. What if I hurt her? Why did they hurt me? What really happened that night? Why did I fail? What if everybody finds out what I've done? Will that mistake come back to haunt me?

They're like big bags of garbage you drag around because you're looking for the right place and the right way to dispose of them. But that makes those uncertainties from the past very much part of the present because of how they limit what you can do and where you can go. If you believe you need to resolve the past before you can move on—that you need to dispose of that garbage in the "right" way—you'll take yourself far off your path in the hope of finding the mythical incinerators of closure and resolution.

Garbage happens. All of the same skills we've discussed about handling uncertainty apply to the past, the present, and the future. It's okay to be uncertain about the past. That doesn't mean we avoid feelings or pretend things didn't happen. Bring compassion and love to those memories so you can loosen your grip on those bags of trash and drop them where they are. Let the pain spill out into the sunlight. We'll explore an exercise for doing that next.

EXERCISE: Healing the Inner Child

These bags of garbage we carry around start getting handed to us when we're young. Maybe somebody you loved told you that you're worthless. He gave you a bag with a little memory of worthlessness rotting inside of it. Carrying that around everywhere started to affect what you did and how you did it. The more garbage you carried, the more it changed how you acted, and the more garbage you got handed to you—failure, shame, regret, embarrassment, guilt. We're not able to be ourselves and do the things we want to do when we're lugging around somebody else's garbage.

For so many years, I thought the way to handle this garbage was to hide it, to avoid going anywhere it might be exposed. I found it all too painful to look at, flinching away from anything that reminded me of that vulnerability. I made excuses to shrink my life so I wouldn't have to deal with it. Learning about and exploring this next meditation exercise helped me find tools to open up those bags, pull out the rotting memories, and embrace them. Through welcoming those vulnerabilities with compassion, it's helped me to make decisions about what I want to let go of and what would actually be useful to take with me on the journey ahead.

This meditation will build on the skills you practiced in the loving-kindness meditation. You'll bring up that warm, loving feeling and take it with you into those difficult emotions and painful memories.

1. Grab a seat and get comfortable. Breathe normally as you gently guide your awareness to the position of your body and the sensation of touch, as we've done with our other meditation practices. Invite your brain to slow down with you.

2. Spend some time meditating like this. Notice what you're feeling and welcome that. You might be anxious about what's coming up. You might start thinking about your

incredibly long to-do list. That's all okay. Gently bring your awareness back to your breath. Notice each inhale. Follow each exhale until it ends. Smile into the brief pause before you inhale again.

3. Take a moment to appreciate your body. Think of something very normal that it's done lately, like helping you carry groceries. Feel gratitude to your body for that. Bring up that feeling of love and kindness you practiced with loving-kindness meditation. Feel that in appreciation of a particular part of your body, or maybe your breath, for keeping you running and living without your even needing to tell it to do anything.

4. Let yourself soak in that appreciation for several breaths. Feel it like it's a gift you're holding. When you're ready, rest that gift in your lap. You'll return to it.

5. Now you'll go back to that time in the past when you felt the pain that's become part of that knot inside of you. It might be an embarrassing situation at school, a time you were scared, a decision you regret, a day you wish you could forget, a moment when somebody you hate said hurtful things to you that you still repeat in your head. Picture the place where the painful event happened. Hear the sounds, smell it, remember what it looked like. Picture any other people who were there.

6. This exercise is partly to practice cognitive defusion. See your current self in that place as well, watching the experience unfold. See your younger self as separate from you. You're going back to this painful place as you are now, knowing what you know now. You're going back to help

that younger version of you. Picture both of your selves there.

7. Remember what that experience felt like for that younger version of you. What did that younger version of you feel at that time? What was racing through your head? What would you say to that younger you? What would you want yourself to know? How can you help that person? How can you bring other people together to help them? What can you share from your experiences over the past couple of years?

8. Give that younger you that gift of gratitude and love and kindness you have with you. Feel yourself expressing it to your younger self. That younger you took on such a big challenge and so much suffering. You know how frightening that was. Extend kindness to that person. You understand why that person still carries this pain. Stay there with that feeling as long as you like. Help her.

9. When you feel like it, hug that younger version of yourself. Encompass her in love and compassion like you're wrapping a bandage around her to help heal the pain. When you feel ready, absorb her inside of you with love. That younger you is still with you. Sit with that awareness of how you got to where you are. Breathe into who you are now.

10. When you're ready, bring your awareness back to the position of your body. Notice your breath, notice how you're in contact with the floor or the seat beneath you. Take some time to breathe. Breathe into that awareness of yourself being in a complex world moving around you. Slowly open your eyes and bring yourself back into contact with your surroundings.

Something to keep in mind as you explore this practice: You might cry. That's okay. You might get very angry. That's okay. Whatever feelings arise are totally okay. There might be many uncomfortable things blocked up behind that knot. You might revisit that particular place several times as you slowly work out this experience. You might uncover other places and experiences you want to practice on as you loosen that knot. It might be very difficult to no longer be fearful and humiliated by that experience, whatever it was. We can't imagine that we're deserving of compassion and love. We can't imagine moving on from them. But all of that is possible.

This is a challenging practice, and if you're struggling with it, go back to working on the loving-kindness meditation. Practice the skills to bring that expression of love into experiences while also feeling pain or guilt or other feelings with which you struggle.

STEP 19

Plan for your wilderness adventure

> I cut out most of my compulsions and began trying to do things proactively instead of reactively, but I still felt very anxious all the time. I realized that acting on my values was something I was doing to try to get rid of anxiety. Letting go of my constant focus on my emotions was the final key to letting go of my remaining anxiety.
>
> —KAMRAN

With each step we take in life, we're moving forward through a fantastic wilderness obstacle course. All of the work we've been doing throughout this book is in service of improving our mental health and emotional fitness so that we can handle any obstacle and keep moving through the wilderness toward our values. On this adventure, we'll swim across lakes, achieve the unthinkable, scale cliffs, admire the beautiful view, hack our way through the undergrowth, prance through meadows, and wrestle beasts that get in our way. This is not going to be an easy hike, so in this chapter we'll explore the five most common barriers I see people running into as they apply the skills we've discussed:

1. Believing you're a unique and special snowflake.
2. Trying to get understanding.
3. Not dismantling the systems in your life built around your compulsions.
4. Mistaking environmental changes for changes in skill or ability.
5. Wanting to avoid relapse.

That fifth one might sound odd but, paradoxically, I think it's the most important barrier to overcome if you're going to avoid relapsing back into the pain, stress, and compulsions that were getting in the way of life. Let's tackle these barriers.

BARRIER #1: BELIEVING YOU'RE A UNIQUE AND SPECIAL SNOWFLAKE

After working with people all over the world on their mental health, I cannot emphasize enough how similar we all are in the mental health challenges we encounter every day, in every culture, across all genders, across social classes, in every imaginable environment. Whatever it is you've been dealing with, I guarantee that people in Port Moresby, Cairo, Bogotá, and Seoul are all dealing with the exact same thing this very minute.

It's also true that we're all running through this obstacle course with our own sets of experiences, privileges, and resources. That can lead to this barrier of believing we're unique in a couple of ways. For instance, your resources may help you overcome some challenges easily. That might make you think you don't need to take care of your mental health like other people—that once you've cut out the compulsions getting in your way, you don't need to deal with the others. You can manage them! You're more capable than other people! But all you've done there is mistaken your resources and privileges for your abilities.

If you experience a change in socioeconomic status, you'll find yourself struggling.

The opposite of that can also happen: You find yourself struggling to leverage a support—something like meditation—or running into a challenge that seems more difficult for you than it does for somebody else. That doesn't necessarily mean there's something unique about your brain that disqualifies you from making use of that support or overcoming that challenge. What you need to look at are things you can change around you that will help you keep moving forward. It's tough to make time for therapy exercises when you're working two jobs to feed your family.

Expect your brain to invent reasons why the adventure ahead is too difficult for you. Also expect it to come up with very convincing arguments as to why you don't need to prepare for the challenges ahead in the same ways that other people do. Don't listen to those reasons or you'll end up going nowhere.

BARRIER #2: TRYING TO GET UNDERSTANDING

You may want to explain to coworkers why you've taken some time off, or you may want society to be more accepting and understanding of mental health issues, or you may want your family to understand how they're making healthy changes more difficult for you. This is all understandable, but it'll still become a barrier because trying to control what other people think is a compulsion. If you try to get understanding from other people, you'll consistently be disappointed, and whatever feeling it was you hoped to get from their understanding will continue to elude you. People can't give you a feeling that comes only from within you. Instead of trying to get understanding, give it. That's going to happen in the form of communication about where you're going.

Imagine you're like a driver in a busy city that has no traffic lights. Compared with most cities in North America, Lisbon, Portugal, has relatively few traffic lights or stop signs at intersections. I was once on the edge of a large park, Jardim do Principe Real, in an older part of the city, and as I crossed the street at a busy intersection, a car turned right, a car came straight through the intersection, and a car turned left all at the exact same time. All three cars were aiming for the same single-lane side street that I and several other pedestrians were crossing at that moment. Everybody had to communicate what they were doing and where they were going. No person in that situation could assume that the other people were going to do what they wanted them to do. We all had potentially conflicting goals but continued safely on our way because we communicated about them.

Life doesn't have traffic lights or stop signs so we need to communicate. Give understanding to where other people are going. Communicate where you're going to those who will play a role in helping you get there.

BARRIER #3: NOT DISMANTLING THE SYSTEMS IN YOUR LIFE BUILT AROUND YOUR COMPULSIONS

One of the biggest challenges to improving our mental health that we can encounter can be the people with whom we've developed relationships with through our compulsions. As you're trying to cut out those compulsions and do things you value, those people will be trying to push you back into the compulsions, sometimes intentionally, sometimes accidentally.

For example, if you were a manager and you engaged in many compulsions micromanaging your staff, you likely built systems in your office that encouraged compulsions and forced people to work in unhealthy ways to cover up your own insecurities. Your staff would be accustomed to that. Their incentives, financial or social, would be aligned with that old way of working. You'd have an entire office of people trying to be life-avoidant rocks. So when you start to change things, they're going to encounter uncertainty and they'll react to that by falling back on what they've done before.

As you make healthy changes, you need to either bring other people with you or recognize that you may no longer be moving forward together. This gets especially complex when you're dealing with romantic or family relationships. We're social animals and losing relationships scares us. If we build relationships around our compulsions but we remove the compulsions, we need to decide if there's a way to build that relationship around something we actually want to keep in our lives.

If you're running into challenges with other people, try doing the Compulsion Journey exercise with a focus on interpersonal relationships to make these systems visible and see opportunities for change.

BARRIER #4: MISTAKING ENVIRONMENTAL CHANGES FOR CHANGES IN SKILL OR ABILITY

Terrain changes. That's a natural part of any journey, whether you're progressing or regressing. Different terrain will require different skills. In a swampy area you might hop from one log to the next. In a steep area you'll climb with all of your limbs and be drenched in sweat when you reach the top. Across a flat meadow you can walk easily.

If you struggled with social anxieties and decided to avoid people by never leaving your house, you'd likely experience a reduction in anxiety (for a short period of time). But that doesn't mean you've learned how to handle your social anxiety issues or that they've gone away. Walking in a circle around a meadow does not mean you know how to climb a mountain.

Conversely, somebody who's progressing along smoothly may encounter an especially difficult environment. That doesn't mean he's developed an illness or lost his abilities. It's very normal to fail initially at something that's new and difficult. Experience that difficulty. It doesn't necessarily mean you've regressed. It might mean you're moving forward and, as part of that, you've encountered a new environment. Understand that environment and the skills you need to develop so you can navigate it effectively.

BARRIER #5: WANTING TO AVOID RELAPSE

When I talk about relapse here, I mean the return of thoughts, feelings, or compulsions that you want to get out of your life. It could be that depression kept you from engaging with your family the way that you wanted to, or you had a panic attack in class, or you struggled with intrusive thoughts that made you question everything in life. Whatever it was, you probably don't want it to happen again. That's understandable. When our mental health isn't in great shape, it's a traumatizing experience.

That's why we do the work we've covered in this book: We learn to experience the stuff in our heads, we cut out compulsions, we make changes in the systems around us, we practice doing the things we value. That all requires a lot of sweaty work, just like improving physical fitness or making any other type of complex change.

As people are doing that work, I get a lot of questions like "So if I cut out these compulsions and start doing more of what matters to me, I won't have this anxiety anymore, right?" But here's what's problematic about a question like that: it takes you back into compulsions. The point of doing these exercises isn't to become a thoughtless, unfeeling rock.

Remember that a compulsion is anything you do to cope with, check on, or control uncertainty, anxiety, and other feelings you don't like. You probably don't want to experience relapse because it will create uncertainty, cause you anxiety, and sink you deep into all sorts of feelings you don't like. But that fear of falling back into those experiences is like any other fear or uncertainty. The moment you start reacting to it and putting it in charge of your life, you've already relapsed, even if you don't feel it yet.

If you truly want to get over a struggle with something like anxiety, stop wanting to avoid it. As long as you're chasing that desire, you're choosing to trap yourself in that experience you hate. This goes back to what we discussed about goals and changing desires. Trying to avoid experiences got you into this struggle. It will not get you out of it. So how do you get out of this trap? Through your actions.

Instead of wanting to avoid relapse, act in a way that builds better mental health. The best defense here is an amazingly devoted, values-based offense in the form of mindful action with each step you take. You don't have to worry about relapse because you have the skills now to handle whatever comes your way. You know how to practice being yourself while experiencing things you don't like. Keep practicing.

ONE MORE EXERCISE

In the final step, I haven't included an exercise. That's because once you're finished reading this book, the only exercise is to continually develop your own personal mental health and fitness lifestyle around the skills and concepts we've explored. But there's one more exercise I want to share with you. It'll combine so much of what you've learned, it'll help you overcome the barriers we just discussed, and it's an exercise you can apply in your life every day. The understanding that comes from this simple exercise has helped me maintain my mental health, continue to improve it, and keep my steps moving through the wilderness of life in a direction that matters to me.

EXERCISE: What's on Your Path?

Now that you're about to apply all of your new emotional fitness skills on this adventure through the wilderness, it'll help to have a map. We don't know exactly what the terrain will be like, however, so this is a map that will help you understand where you are based on the mental and physical actions you're engaging in at any moment. Those actions are your steps. You can know whether you're wandering off the path based on the steps you're taking.

Hopefully you have a clear understanding now of the actions that would indicate that you're way off the path and stuck waist-deep in a bog. And you understand what you value and how your values translate into actions. Those are the steps that are clearly on the path. The value of this exercise we're going to do now is in articulating the actions that are just off your path. Those are going to be the seemingly "normal" compulsions that might not bother you but that you've seen are indicators that you're heading off in the wrong direction. By understanding the actions that are just a few steps off the path, you can empower yourself to spot problems sooner and correct course. This is all part of being proactive and taking a values-based approach to your journey. We don't have to wait until we're lost to understand the value of sticking to what matters to us.

1. Divide a piece of paper into three columns. Label the columns "On the Path," "Just off the Path," and "Way off the Path."

2. List the actions that go in each column. What are you going to do each day to be healthy and happy and work toward your goals in life? List all of that in the "On the Path" column. What are the things you do that you consider totally misaligned with who you are and where you want to be in life? Put all of that under "Way off the Path." What are the actions that set you up for or contribute to your going way off the path? That's what goes under "Just off the Path."

3. You'll probably work on this list several times as you learn more about what sinks you into unhealthy behaviors.

4. Be as specific as you can be about the actions you list. For example, instead of writing something like "Not avoiding triggers," you can consider what the triggers are and list the actions that will take you directly into them, like "Articulating my opinions in meetings," or "Getting changed in front of others in the locker room," or "Babysitting my friends' kids."

5. Note that the actions in each column don't necessarily need to correlate across the columns. You might see some direct connections but that's not always the case. These actions are indicators, like sensors in your life telling you where you are. I'll share an example of some actions I would put in those three columns and you'll see what I mean:

ON THE PATH	JUST OFF THE PATH	WAY OFF THE PATH
• Volunteering • Going to the gym 5x per week and consistently challenging myself to learn new skills, lift more, or go further • Cooking 90 percent of my own meals • Using social media to help people • Creating work I care about and sharing it publicly • Collaborating with others and not working alone • Sharing my meditation practice with others • Hosting friends at my home and feeding them • Intentionally spending time with family for no particular reason • Going to a new place or doing something new in my city at least once per month • Setting aside time each month to experience nature and care for it	• Procrastinating on laundry, taking out the garbage, or cleaning • Investing hours and hours in obsessing over relationships and hunting for dates • Buying breakfasts at restaurants (because I didn't get groceries or take time to make my breakfast the night before) • Staying up late on my phone in bed • Flipping through social media mindlessly • Making excuses to not meditate • Not tracking my budget • Refreshing my blog or e-mail account to check for responses to posts or messages • Spending hours watching series I don't like much • Eating all of the chocolate in my cupboards • Weighing myself	• Checking doors, windows, locks, taps, appliances, etc. • Lying to people • Getting into a relationship to escape loneliness • Missing out on sleep because I stayed up all night online • Not using knives • Reacting to fears of being poisoned, watched, or attacked • Always waiting for friends to contact me first • Asking for reassurance from my friends and family • Researching illness symptoms online • Quitting jobs, changing careers, and changing cities every year or so • Paying bills or taxes late • Not showering or shaving • Buying expensive appliances I don't need and don't use

Keep taking steps

I was afraid to speak publicly about my mental health challenges, but once I did, I was surprised to learn that a couple of friends were going through something similar. I was so relieved that I wasn't alone and we could now have conversations about this important aspect of our lives.

—ANNIE

You now have at your disposal the knowledge to help you build your own mental health and emotional fitness practice. You **understand that you are not a rock,** you're a human, so you feel things and think things. Sometimes you won't like those things, sometimes you'll love them, but when you're struggling, you won't get caught chasing after them. Instead, you'll **recognize your problems** and go after them, even when that requires complex changes in your life or the environment around you. As you work on those changes, you'll **practice mindfulness** and you'll **meditate** so you can build the capacity to experience whatever you're experiencing as you **follow your values.** That'll require you to **focus on changing actions, not thoughts or feelings.** No longer trying to change thoughts or feelings will mean you can stop compulsions. You'll **stop coping** and you'll **break your IF X THEN Y thinking pattern** so you can free yourself from the equations that keep you trapped in anxiety and stress. You'll **stop checking** and **you'll understand your fears** by digging into the reasons behind your compulsions so you can uncover the issues you actually need to practice accepting. You'll **stop controlling** other people, your internal experiences, the past, and the future. That'll be possible because you'll **tame the monster** of urges and fears in your head that throws uncertainties at you to trick you into feeding it compulsions. This will all lead to a major transformation in your life as you **switch your life's fuel from fear to values.** But don't go looking for motivation to make the switch. So you'll need to **break your motivation addiction.** Chasing that feeling is like chasing any other feeling. You might believe that motivation is necessary but that'll be just one of the beliefs you end up ditching. To succeed at sticking to your values you'll need to **throw out unhelpful beliefs and desires.** And you'll have the opportunity to rewrite your beliefs and desires every time you accept an experience, **practice nonjudgment,** and choose actions aligned with your values. You can show your brain your beliefs through your actions as you **make happiness a practice,** recognizing that it's a skill that comes only after regular, often challenging practice. Doing those things that actually make you happy, the things that matter to you in life, will require you to **embrace uncertainty** to an extent you probably never have before. That's part of innovating and exploring new territory. You're venturing into uncharted wilderness in your life, so **plan for your wilderness adventure.** Support the work of living by your values as you combine all of these skills into the present moment and **keep taking steps** in the direction of your values.

The practice of accepting the stuff in your head and doing things you value is one you can enjoy every day for the rest of your life. There will be days when you struggle with that practice. There will be bad days, and terrible days, and absolutely horrible days. Make space for them. Feel them. You can trust yourself to experience them. In the present moment—the only place you can possibly be—you can always make a choice about how you act. As you become more skilled at making choices, you'll see that acting according to your values isn't only about yourself. It's about your community.

GO BEYOND YOU

There are many misconceptions about mindfulness and meditation, one of those being that they're solitary, self-focused practices, above the world and its troubles, things you do while hiding away in a hut up on a mountain cultivating pristine balance. But hopefully you've seen that these practices aren't about avoiding the world or feelings you don't like. These practices are about diving headfirst into those experiences and swimming around in them to support long-term health and happiness. The fact is, your health is connected to your environment and the communities of people with which you interact, virtually and in the real world. Because of those multifaceted connections, you cannot build health and happiness without working on it at the community level—even the global level—alongside and connected to the changes you'll work on as an individual. Your health, comprised of your physical and mental health, is not separate from your neighbors' health, the health of your public institutions, the health of the water systems you depend upon, or the financial health of the young woman who picked the tomato you ate in your salad for lunch.

In the same way that you can't be surprised if your mental health falls apart when you haven't been taking care of it, you can't be surprised if your community, your company, or your government is falling apart when all you've done to care for it is shout your complaints and indignation on social media as a way to signal to your in-group that you have the right opinions, just like they do.

It's fine if you have judgments. They happen. But what matters are your actions.

How can you push into the fear and uncertainty around you and help your community not react to them with controlling compulsions like racism, sexism, xenophobia, homophobia, transphobia, or any other type of bigotry? How can you instead create an inclusive, equitable community through your collaborative actions?

On project teams at school or at work, how can you help people stick to values instead of falling back into the same old habits when they get anxious working up that Unhappiness Curve?

How can you help the organizations you're a part of not react to anxiety with decisions that provide short-term relief at the long-term expense of the organization's health and well-being? How can you help your organization go beyond a self-centered focus to support its community or the environment?

You're not going to wait until you end up in a hospital psychiatric unit to start taking care of your mental health, so why wait until your water is contaminated and undrinkable to start caring for the environment? What proactive actions can you take to maintain and improve our natural environment?

Critically examine your beliefs, judgments, and desires connected to systems beyond you. Are your beliefs helping you? Are they helping your community? Maybe you're wrong about some people or some issues. Maybe you're putting your time and energy into things that won't actually lead to the outcomes you want to see.

And how are you going to interact with your community around mental health issues? Will you try to hide the challenges you've had with your brain because you're afraid of what people might think?

THE FEAR OF STIGMA IS LIKE
ANY OTHER FEAR

With all of the changes we've explored in this book, people are going to notice that you're doing things differently. You won't be walking around with a liter of hand sanitizer in your purse. You'll speak up in situations when you would've stayed quiet in the past. You might say no more often. Maybe you'll stop being that friend who always cancels at the last minute. You'll be able to handle emotions better, so you won't lash out abusively at people. You'll also be able to express affection honestly—you can tell your date you like her without waiting three days to send an indifferent, passive-aggressive message because you're afraid of coming on too strong. Maybe you'll take lessons to learn a new skill you've been procrastinating on for years. You'll be interacting with new people and old friends in new ways. There might be some relationships that aren't part of your life anymore.

People will either ask about what's happening or you'll want to talk to them about these changes because they're affected by them. So here are two things to consider that I've learned from talking about my brain:

1. **If you react to the fear of stigma, expect it to lead to the same natural consequences you'd experience by reacting to any fear: more anxiety, more fear, lots of uncertainty, a shrinking life.** There are situations with very real consequences to speaking openly about mental health struggles. In those situations, you need to decide between those consequences and the consequences you'll experience by remaining silent. It's alarming that people can lose their jobs or be ostracized for speaking honestly about common experiences that so many others around them are struggling with silently in shame. That's one of the reasons why those who can speak openly need to engage with making healthy changes throughout their communities, at work, or in public policy. You can't have great mental health if you're reacting to the fear of speaking openly about your mental health, so we need to make that possible for everybody, everywhere.

   Having said that . . .

2. **Talk about mental health in the same way you talk about physical fitness.** When you get an urge to avoid a friend's event because of anxiety but you go to support your friend, you're exercising. It's

like going for a run or lifting weights. When you commit to experiencing more uncertainty in a relationship and you take simple steps each day to build a healthy relationship, that's like somebody who starts working on the skills to compete in his first triathlon even though it's several months away. You're building your health. It's not about illness.

Talk about where you're going and what you're building. Like we discussed in the introduction: If you're going to the gym to build strength, you don't label yourself as having a weakness disorder. You've recognized challenges you have with emotions and you're developing the skills and abilities to handle those emotions while doing things you love. That is the most awesomely wonderful thing imaginable. Talk about that. Engage people around doing what you love. They can join you in building health for yourself and for your community.

BRAINS ARE CHRONIC

There was a time when physical exercise was something that only soldiers, sick people, and professional athletes did. Jogging or working out at a gym was highly unusual. If you'd been in any large city in the 1970s and seen a man running down the street in a pair of short shorts and a tank top, you probably would've assumed he had hopped out of a window and was running away in his underwear from his lover's jealous husband.

Now, all over the world, it's quite common to live near a weight-lifting gym or to pass groups of people out jogging in the morning (if you wake up early enough to see them). You can easily find workout plans online, you can follow along at home to free yoga instructional videos, and you don't have to pay an expensive doctor to exercise with you. You most certainly don't need to be on a wait list for nine months waiting for somebody to tell you how to exercise.

We've made physical fitness accessible. We have to do the same with mental health, for everybody, because everybody has a brain, and those delicate imagination organs jiggling around in our skulls are chronic.

You'll have mental health as long as you have a brain, just as you'll have physical health as long as you have a body. Your physical health and your mental health will vary but you can take steps to proactively maintain and improve both of them. The practice of caring for your health is a lifestyle, it's a way of living. It's not a magic pill, an app, a device, or a mantra. It's a way of doing what you do, wherever you are, wherever you're going.

This won't be the last book you read about mental health. The exercises we've covered won't be the last exercises you learn. But I hope this is the beginning of a journey for you, a journey of many steps, as you push into difficult experiences, building and increasing your emotional fitness level, moving in the direction of your values, up and over many challenges along the way. As you take those steps, remember to breathe. If you stumble off the path on your journey, breathe. In the present, you can always take a step aligned with your values. That next step is the one that matters. The step you take now. In what direction will you step? Where are you going?

WHERE ARE YOU GOING?

NOTES

INTRODUCTION

5 **fifty burpees:** Thanks to Blair and everybody at CrossFit YKV for telling me to pick up the bar when I think I can't. And for including burpees in workouts, even though burpees are wrong.

8 **be less reactive:** Els van der Helm et al., "REM Sleep Depotentiates Amygdala Activity to Previous Emotional Experiences," *Current Biology* 21, no. 23 (December 2011): 2029–32, doi:10.1016/j.cub.2011.10.052.

9 **they recover from schizophrenia:** When I bring up the topic of recovery from mental illness, I often hear things like "Sure, but not with something like schizophrenia, right?" That kind of question, however, expresses only the stigma we've attached to the schizophrenia label for too long. People with lived experience of psychosis have been leading the recovery movement for decades, and research shows that between 40 percent and 60 percent of patients can expect remission through current clinical treatments: Martin Lambert et al., "Remission in Schizophrenia: Validity, Frequency, Predictors, and Patients' Perspective 5 Years Later," *Dialogues in Clinical Neuroscience* 12, no. 3 (September 2010): 393–407.

9   **they recover from borderline personality disorder:** Over the course of ten years, 83 percent of participants in this study experienced remission of symptoms lasting at least four years, and 50 percent of patients achieved recovery: Mary C. Zanarini et al., "Time to Attainment of Recovery from Borderline Personality Disorder and Stability of Recovery: A 10-Year Prospective Follow-up Study," *American Journal of Psychiatry* 167, no. 6 (June 2010): 663–67, doi:10.1176/appi.ajp.2009.09081130.

10   **they recover from eating disorders:** Forty-nine percent of patients seeking treatment achieved recovery over the course of this study: David B. Herzog et al., "Recovery and Relapse in Anorexia and Bulimia Nervosa: A 7.5-Year Follow-up Study," *Journal of the American Academy of Child & Adolescent Psychiatry* 38, no. 7 (July 1999): 829–37, doi:10.1097/00004583-199907000-00012.

10   **they recover from depression:** This meta-analysis of ninety-two studies on psychotherapy for major depressive disorder (MDD), encompassing 6,937 patients, found that 62 percent of patients no longer met the criteria for MDD after therapy: Pim Cuijpers et al., "The Effects of Psychotherapies for Major Depression in Adults on Remission, Recovery and Improvement: A Meta-analysis," *Journal of Affective Disorders* 159 (April 2014): 118–26, doi:10.1016/j.jad.2014.02.026.

10   **they recover from addiction:** Of 4,422 adults with a history of alcohol dependence, 35.9 percent were in complete recovery and 27.3 percent were in partial remission: Deborah A. Dawson et al., "Recovery from DSM-IV Alcohol Dependence: United States, 2001–2002," *Addiction* 100, no. 3 (March 2005): 281–92, doi:10.1111/j.1360-0443.2004.00964.x.

10   **it doesn't happen through magic:** The recovery rates in the studies

mentioned above might not seem high, but consider this: Therapy isn't something that happens to you. It's something you do. A therapist can advise a patient on what to do, but the patient has to do it. It's no different from a personal trainer giving a weekly exercise program to a client. If the client doesn't exercise, nothing happens. Those rates of recovery might even be high given what we normally see when people are making major personal changes. What percentage of people at your gym in January are still there in July? How many people who go to the gym regularly achieve their fitness goals?

STEP 1: UNDERSTAND THAT YOU ARE NOT A ROCK

18   You are not like that rock: When I was writing this book, you could still see two of the rocks on Google Maps by visiting these coordinates: 46°19'22.5"N 11°14'02.0"E.

STEP 3: PRACTICE MINDFULNESS

36   "the awareness that arises through paying attention": Maia Szalavitz, "Q&A: Jon Kabat-Zinn Talks About Bringing Mindfulness Meditation to Medicine," *Time*, January 11, 2012.

STEP 4: MEDITATE

48   increase gray matter density: Britta K. Hölzel et al., "Mindfulness Practice Leads to Increases in Regional Brain Gray Matter Density," *Psychiatry Research: Neuroimaging* 191, no. 1 (January 2011): 36–43, doi:10.1016/j.pscychresns.2010.08.006.

49   sensory awareness and executive decision making: Sara W. Lazar et al., "Meditation Experience Is Associated with Increased Cortical Thickness," *NeuroReport* 16, no. 17 (November 2005):

1893–97, doi:10.1097/01.wnr.0000186598.66243.19. Keep in mind (no pun intended) that these studies drawing a connection between meditation and physical changes in the brain don't tell us anything about what those changes mean. What I take away from any studies like these is simply that repetitive actions can impact my brain. So it reminds me to be considerate of the actions I do repeatedly in my life.

49 **less emotionally triggered:** Catherine N. M. Ortner et al., "Mindfulness Meditation and Reduced Emotional Interference on a Cognitive Task," *Motivation and Emotion* 31, no. 4 (December 2007): 271–83, doi:10.1007/s11031-007-9076-7.

49 **keep your mind from wandering off:** Michael D. Mrazek et al., "Mindfulness Training Improves Working Memory Capacity and GRE Performance While Reducing Mind Wandering," *Psychological Science* 24, no. 5 (May 2013): 776–81, doi:10.1177/0956797612459659.

STEP 6: FOCUS ON CHANGING ACTIONS, NOT THOUGHTS OR FEELINGS

77 **fill in the blanks with any combination:** Let's fill in the blanks with a specific example:

You can create a simple grid to help with exploring how experiences in your life turn into compulsions. Here are some examples:

WHAT DID YOU EXPERIENCE?	HOW DO YOU JUDGE THAT EXPERIENCE?	WHAT DOES THAT MAKE YOU FEEL?	WHAT DO YOU WANT?	WHAT DO YOU DO AS A REACTION TO THAT DESIRE?
I failed on a work project.	It's embarrassing.	I'm afraid other people will think I'm incompetent.	I want them to see they're still worse than me.	I publicly criticize others so the focus is on their faults.
I stepped on a strange-looking stain on the street.	It was dangerous and mindless.	I'm worried I picked up something toxic on my brand-new shoes.	I want to be certain I won't contaminate anybody else.	I put my shoes in a bag and stick them in a closetful of clothes I avoid.
Everything in my life is going so perfectly.	It's amazing. It's like the universe is working for me.	I'm irritated by people trying to hold me back from my full potential.	I want people to see how I can attract abundance.	I take my family's life savings to the casino. . . .
School was incredibly stressful today.	I don't deserve to feel so stressed.	I'm anxious this feeling will interfere with my plans for the night.	I want to replace this feeling with a better one.	I eat half of a pie I was going to take to a dinner party.
I saw an image in my head of somebody I know getting hurt.	That shouldn't have been in my head.	I'm worried that having a thought like that means I could hurt people.	I want to be certain I'm disgusted by the thought of hurting people.	I spend hours thinking through my memories to make sure I've never hurt anybody and would be horrified by that possibility.

STEP 7: STOP COPING

87 **being sedentary increases your risk of disease:** I hope you're not sitting down, but this meta-analysis, examining studies that encompassed hundreds of thousands of patients, found that being sedentary increases your risk for all-cause mortality, cancer mortality, cardiovascular disease mortality, and rates of cancer, cardiovascular disease, and type 2 diabetes: Aviroop Biswas et al., "Sedentary Time and Its Association with Risk for Disease Incidence, Mortality, and Hospitalization in Adults: A Systematic Review and Meta-analysis," *Annals of Internal Medicine* 162, no. 2 (January 2015): 123–32, doi:10.7326/m14-1651.

89 **psychological flexibility:** It's "the ability to fully contact the present moment and the thoughts and feelings it contains without needless defense, and to persist in or change behavior, depending on the situation, in the pursuit of goals and values." From Joseph Ciarrochi et al., "Psychological Flexibility as a Mechanism of Change in Acceptance and Commitment Therapy," in *Assessing Mindfulness and Acceptance Processes in Clients: Illuminating the Theory and Practice of Change*, ed. Ruth A. Baer (Oakland, CA: Context Press, 2010), 51–76.

89 **"Accept your reactions and be present":** Steven C. Hayes et al., *Acceptance and Commitment Therapy: An Experiential Approach to Behavior Change* (New York: Guilford Press, 1999), 246.

STEP 9: STOP CHECKING

114 **"cause clinically significant distress":** *Diagnostic and Statistical Manual of Mental Disorders, 5th ed.* (Washington, DC: American Psychiatric Association, 2013), 237.

STEP 11: STOP CONTROLLING

130 **The man dies:** Franz Kafka, *The Trial*, trans. Willa Muir and Edwin Muir (New York: Schocken Books, 1995), 213. You can also find this as a stand-alone story, titled "Before the Law," in many collections of Kafka's short stories.

STEP 12: TAME THE MONSTER

147 **passengers on a bus:** Steven C. Hayes and Spencer Smith, "What Are Values?" chap. 11 in *Get Out of Your Mind and Into Your Life: The New Acceptance and Commitment Therapy* (Oakland, CA: New Harbinger Publications, 2005), 153.

147 **demons on a boat:** Russ Harris, "Demons on the Boat," chap. 9 in *The Happiness Trap: How to Stop Struggling and Start Living* (Boston: Trumpeter Books, 2008), 76.

STEP 13: SWITCH THE FUEL FOR LIFE FROM FEAR TO VALUES

162 **one in five people will experience a mental illness:** Center for Behavioral Health Statistics and Quality, *Behavioral Health Trends in the United States: Results from the 2014 National Survey on Drug Use and Health*, HHS Publication No. SMA 15-4927, NSDUH Series H-50, 2015.

162 **lifetime prevalence of experiencing a mental illness:** Ronald C. Kessler et al., "Lifetime Prevalence and Age-of-Onset Distributions of DSM-IV Disorders in the National Comorbidity Survey Replication," *Archives of General Psychiatry* 62, no. 6 (June 2005): 593–602, doi:10.1001/archpsyc.62.6.593.

STEP 15: THROW OUT UNHELPFUL BELIEFS AND DESIRES

189   the experience of having the panic attack: David H. Barlow, *Anxiety and Its Disorders: The Nature and Treatment of Anxiety and Panic* (New York: Guilford Press, 1988), 240.

STEP 16: PRACTICE NONJUDGMENT

199   "Are you sure of your perceptions?": Thich Nhat Hanh, *You Are Here: Discovering the Magic of the Present Moment*, trans. Sherab Chödzin Kohn (Boston: Shambhala Publications, 2009), 99.

INDEX

Note: Page numbers in *italics* refer to illustrations.

and Practicing Not Feeling Right
    exercise, 178–80
empowerment, 9–10, 65
enemies, struggling with, 205–6
environment, natural, 241
environmental changes, 228
Everybody Has a Brain online
    community, 143
exercising
    changing behaviors related to, 171
    as coping behavior, 87
    and emotional fitness, 8
exposure and response prevention
    (ERP) therapy, 62–63, 80–83

failing
    feelings of, 207–8
    as normal experience, 231–32
    role of, in growth, 5–6
fears, 122–28, 153–67
    and ACT model, 115
    attempting to control, 26–27,
        67–68
    and cleaning behaviors, 159–60
    and clothing/grooming
        behaviors, 158
    and cognitive defusion, 142
    conflating self with, 141
    and eliminating compulsions, 93
    and happiness, 205
    personal responsibility in lieu
        of, 163
    in relationships, 158–59
    and social media, 157
    and Stockholm Syndrome, 206–7
    and unreasonableness, 176
    and value-based actions/approach,
        65, 66–68, 155, 164–67,
        200, 207
    in work or school settings, 156
feedback loops related to
    uncertainty, 112–13
Five Whys exercise, 126–28, 199
flow, 184

food choices
    and emotional fitness, 7–8
    and gratitude practices, 212
    and Practicing Not Feeling Right
        exercise, 179
functioning, tracking, 207–9

generalized anxiety disorder (GAD),
    3, 114
Get Out of Your Mind and into
    Your Life (Hayes and
    Smith), 147
giving and getting, 157
goals
    and Creative Human Goals
        exercise, 20–22
    guidelines for, 172
    for rocks vs. humans, 19–22
gratitude practices, 210–12
grooming habits, 158, 211
guilt, choosing to feel, 88

hand washing, 160
happiness, 204–15
    and avoiding unhappiness, 20
    and battling internal enemies,
        205–6
    and coping behaviors, 84
    and emotions/feelings, 207–9
    fear-fueled approach to, 205
    functioning as measure of,
        207–9
    and gratitude practices, 210–12
    and Loving-Kindness Meditation,
        212–15
    practice required for, 209–10
    and Stockholm Syndrome, 206–7
    and values, 208
The Happiness Trap (Harris), 147
Harris, Russ, 147
hating, endurance in, 209–10
Hayes, Steven C.
    and ACT model, 89, 90, 147
    on good mental health, 163–64